To Prof Igor An...
with appreciati...

[signature]

Alexander J. Ayy...

San Diego
July 28, 1994

Vision Into Action

The Leader's Guide to Driving Change in Turbulent Times

TERO J. KAUPPINEN
ALEXANDER J. OGG, JR.

Leadership Studies International, Inc.
San Diego, California

International Standard Book Number: 0-9640787-0-8

Library of Congress Catalog Card Number: 94-075981

Printed in the United States of America

Library of Congress Cataloging-in-Publication Data
Kauppinen, Tero, 1949
Ogg, Alexander, 1954
        Via: The Leader's Guide to Driving Change in
        Turbulent Times/Tero Kauppinen and Alexander Ogg.
        p. cm.
        ISBN 0-9640787-0-8
        1. Leadership   2. Transformation   3. Change
        4. Management   I. Title

DEDICATION

This book is dedicated to friendship,
the necessary ingredient for success
in many of our strategic partnerships,
without which this book
would never have been written.

Especially, this book is dedicated to
Robyn and Tiia,
our strategic partners in life.
You have brought good things into our lives.

Finally, to our parents,
Matti and Liisa, Alexander and Kathryn,
who provided the strong roots
that have helped us to grow this far.

Contents

Preface

A Guided Tour
For Your Reading
Experience

*Excellent performance
rarely happens by accident.*

Dewey Johnson
Professor of Leadership and
Strategic Management,

Fresno State University,
California

A leader's job is
to organize success

Regardless of the change that has occurred in the environment and in organizations, a leader's job has never changed; it has always been to *organize success*. However, excelling in that role has become increasingly exacting and difficult. Demands from a multitude of constituencies and the need for a wide variety of skills require that today's leaders exhibit an uncommon mixture of abilities and wisdom. This mix includes the creativity to adapt to new and novel situations, and a capacity for seeing beyond the obvious to opportunities that lie on the other side of conventional wisdom.

> **In an age of discontinuous change,
> managers must learn to deal with "breakpoints"
> —sudden changes in the rules of the game
> that redefine competition and
> organizational behavior.**
> **Paul Strebel**

Unfortunately, most planning, strategizing and implementation in organizations is not geared to today's competitive atmosphere. Previous achievements create habits and beliefs that cause leaders to repeat their old, successful formulas, no matter how invalid in their current business environments.

> **Leadership depends on the ability
> to frame issues correctly—that is to answer
> the question, "What is <u>really</u> going on?"**
> **Robert W. Terry**

Other leaders are painfully aware of the mismatches between their business and the key players surrounding it, or between necessary strategies and current organizational culture. They condition themselves to *ignore* opportunities that their organizations obviously cannot pursue—even if they know that success demands a different approach.

In the stable, traditional managerial era, one did not need to know how to deal with new challenges like cultural change, the horizontal organization or empowerment of the work force. In those days, organizations were designed to excel in a fairly placid, continuously-growing environment. Span of control was limited, and reliability and economies of scale were the success factors. Tools like Management By Objectives, based on an annual rhythm, were popular and organizations grew in size and became multilayered bureaucracies. For example, in 1981, General Electric still had a total of 29 layers.

But turbulence grew and old ways ceased to work. New approaches emerged as *the* solution. Total Quality Management, re-engineering, the concept of the learning organization, cycle time reduction, the ubiquitous "right sizing"—all have been tried as means to keep organizations afloat and avoid corporate pain. Returning to our previous example, by 1992 GE had reduced its organization by 20 layers and was planning to flatten even more—to only five management levels.

However, as worthwhile as many of these approaches are, turbulence has consequences that they cannot address. Reactive resistance to change, a distrust of personal instincts, the nagging suspicion that "nothing will change for the better,"—all create an atmosphere of almost fatalistic resignation, and an inability to think creatively in the midst of seeming chaos.

The current key to success lies in making leaders and their organizations *ready for change,* capable of finding *stability in the midst of the turbulence,* and sufficiently *robust*, through the development of self-perpetuating processes, to weather any storm.

Change is an inevitable, unstoppable reality. It must become a way of life for today's organizations. Leaders must step outside of their customary ways of seeing and doing in order to develop the competencies to win in the new reality. And they must do so quickly. That is the premise on which this book is based.

The diagram on the next page: *Via: Vision Into Action* is designed to help you navigate through this book's four parts and ten chapters. Each part addresses an aspect of orchestrating change in our turbulent times.

Via: Vision Into Action

PART ONE
Turbulent Times

Chapter 1
**Turbulence:
The White Water
Decade**

Chapter 2
**Measuring
the Waves**

Chapter 3
**Creating
Renewable
Competitive
Advantage**

PART TWO
The Leader's Guide

Chapter 4
**From
Vision Into Action**

PART THREE
Driving Change

VISIONARY LEVEL
Chapter 5
Creating the Future
Chapter 6
Visionary Leadership

STRATEGIC LEVEL
Chapter 7
**Strategic Leadership:
The Change Engines**

TEAM LEVEL
Chapter 8
**Team Leadership:
Making It Work**

INDIVIDUAL LEVEL
Chapter 9
**Personal Transformation:
Via My Way**

PART FOUR
The Challenge

Chapter 10
**Your
Personal
Challenge**

Our first three chapters discuss the aspects of the current operating environment that have created such turbulence and discontinuous change. Utilizing a number of different metaphors, **Chapter One** illustrates the current "white water decade." **Chapter Two**, defines and measures environmental turbulence and the ways in which businesses have responded. **Chapter Three** introduces the concept of "renewable competitive advantage." We utilize the term renewable —as opposed to sustainable—in recognition of the fact that a sustained advantage connotes a static or slowly evolving business setting. What we seek is advantage that can continuously adapt to change.

Chapter Four introduces the Via Model, our framework for diagnosis, intervention, and the creation of renewable competitive advantage. It covers in detail the unique aspects of the model—a distillation of the "best of the best" leadership theories and a pairing of both the business and people sides of organizational life.

Creating the future and visionary leadership are covered in **Chapters Five** and **Six**. The importance of organizational mission and vision is emphasized, and the concept of "whole brain visioning" is introduced. **Chapter Six** is particularly pertinent for senior executives and agents of change. Within this chapter we address the importance of a business' key players and the role of the visionary leader.

> **The New Competition is causing organizations to redefine their relationships with vendors, customers and even competitors...**
> **they are seeking more collaborative relationships that will bind them into networks.**
> **Nitin Nohria**

Chapter Seven discusses the leadership of organizational transformation. Where visionary leadership takes the high view of the future in the business environment, strategic leadership addresses the future of the organization itself. Within this context we elaborate on the concept of the *Via Change Engine*, a systems approach to change management and a self-perpetuating combination of the "best of the best" in organizational transformation technology today.

In **Chapter Eight** we speak of the importance of teams. Teams are not a fad. They are a reality of organizational life as the pace of change increases. We must begin to see them as tools, much as we view information systems as tools, to be managed and led. A good match between a team and its goals leads to clear individual roles and responsibilities, which are essential for success. Via *TeamTools* and *Leadership Tools*, two pieces of our organizational *ChangeTools* kit, can facilitate this success.

Personal transformation is the topic of **Chapter Nine**. This may seem odd in a leader's guide for driving organizational change, but it is important to realize that leaders must understand human thinking and motivation and be able to assist individuals in making work meaningful. The flattening of organizational structures, the increased breadth of span of control, the increase in team structures, and growing employee demand for meaningful work have handicapped traditional supervision. The new worker will be internally motivated and self-led. However, moving towards this "inside out" way of viewing one's destiny is difficult, hence the development of the *Via My Way* model.

> **It is essential to develop a new leadership theory and practice that incorporates the authenticity, the ethical sensibility and the spirituality needed by leaders if their work is to be relevant to today's problems.**
> **Robert W. Terry**

Finally, **Chapter Ten** is both challenge and invitation: a challenge to effective leadership that addresses both organizational survival and individual need, and an invitation to search for that effectiveness through Via as a framework.

> **The most adaptive part of a system controls that system.**

Acknowledgments

"No one can succeed alone."

Acknowledging our value base.

We wish to first acknowledge the special partnership that was created when we established our company, the Via Consulting Group. It was the first time either of us had ever entered into a partnership by first conducting a *value audit*. Our common values have been the basis for our friendship and the glue that has held us together through turbulent and changing times. It has been the foundation for creativity, for daring moves, and for writing this book.

Acknowledging the prime driver—our customers.

It is very important for a consultant to win the trust of some first-rate companies, those which have already done many of the right things to make themselves leaders in their industries. These companies challenge consultants to stretch and ask them to walk the roads less traveled and to blaze new trails.

Our clients have pushed us to create new approaches. For that, we thank them.

We want to mention some of the organizations that, over the years, have contributed to the development of many of the concepts presented in this book: Motorola, whose contributions are evident throughout the book; General Electric, which has set an inspiring example; Kaiser Aluminum, where we conducted our first joint project; Northern Telecom, where we learned a great deal and numerous others. Some international companies which have contributed to our work in special ways include Caltex in Australia, and

Southeast Asia, Haka-Auto, which imports Jaguar and Mazda automobiles to Finland, and Valmet, the world leader in paper manufacturing machines. Even some smaller family-owned businesses have been incubators of our ideas: Halton, Ltd. and Timosaurus, Ltd.

Our thanks to those who have kicked us in the right places at the right times.

When one is kicked, it is often difficult to see the lesson hidden in the pain. However, we want to thank our competitors, some tough customers, and our friends for giving us a swift one when we needed it.

There are many thought leaders who have shaped our thinking.

Books and articles by various thinkers and writers have taught us a lot. We have attempted to give them appropriate credit in the text and references. However, it is impossible to mention all of the contributors to this book since some of their teachings are so deeply internalized that we no longer recognize the original sources. Thank you all for your contributions to our thinking and writing.

Certain individuals have strongly influenced us and we want to acknowledge their contribution. Our guru and teacher in the area of leadership has been *Dr. Paul Hersey*, who taught us more about leadership than anyone else. The late *Voitto Talonen*, a genuine visionary leader himself, taught us the importance of visions. *Dr. Robert C. Rommel* showed us the importance of simultaneously combining business and human behavioral issues in our work. *Professor Warren Bennis* helped us to see the leader's role in a new light. We borrowed from *Professor Igor Ansoff's* strategic mind to inspire our own strategic thinking. *Professor Dewey Johnson* and *Professor Asko Miettinen* have acted as our coaches, helping us to shape and clarify our thinking, and discussions with *Professor Jim Belasco* provided inspiring views of what the right kind of organizational intervention could accomplish—teaching elephants to dance and buffaloes to fly. *Professor Harold Cheatham* first introduced, and gave Sandy a love for, the behavioral sciences.

Many practical leaders have set personal examples and/or provided thoughts and ideas that are presented in this book.

Chris Galvin, president of Motorola, provided many ideas and concepts. The leadership philosophy of *John Lockitt*, former president of Motorola Codex gave us a lot of food for thought. The entrepreneurial approach to leading a company was elaborated by *Mike Birck* CEO of Tellabs. *George Fisher*, CEO of Kodak, taught us the value of uncompromising integrity in everything we do. *Jim Donnelly*, Executive Vice President of Human Resources at Motorola, taught us to maintain the courage of our own convictions and devotion to family. *Pekka Prättälä*, former CEO of Keskimaa, demonstrated people leadership in practice. *Martti Kemppi*, founder and Chairman of Kemppi Oy, one of the largest welding machinery manufacturers in Europe, taught us that caring and serving should be the heart of leadership tools and models. *Seppo Halttunen*, Chairman of the Halton Group, showed us the value of bold leadership and counterintuitive action in achieving extraordinary results.

There are many others. Some even showed us through their examples what *not* to do, which is equally important.

We could not have been effective with our clients without constant dialogue and interaction with our coaches, our in-house counterparts on projects.

Project experience forms the backbone of the ideas presented in this book. We want to acknowledge the important input of corporate specialists such as *Rick Canada, Joe Miraglia* and *Pat Canavan* of Motorola, *Eero Leivo* and *Jukka Aho* of Valmet, *Dan Stolle* of Tellabs and *Don Gillies* of Caltex. Without their guidance we would not have made it this far.

Our colleagues in the Via Consulting Network have made significant contributions to this book.

We would like to give special thanks to the Finnish team at Yritysvalmennus Group, who, over several years, have tested, implemented and given feedback on Via instruments, tools and programs. Their input has been crucial in the development of the ideas in this book and in testing them in global settings, including Russia. *Matti Virkki, Rauno Janhunen, Hannu Kunttu, Reijo Kaikkonen, Tero Järvinen, Hannele Piispanen, Jukka Alava, Pertti Laamanen, Niilo Nylander* and *Risto Kauppinen* have all contributed in meaningful ways.

The active dialogue and feedback of *Gustav Pansegrouw* and his colleagues in South Africa, *Doug Long* of Australia, *Bo Gyllenpalm* of Sweden, *Jose Cabrera* of Mexico and *Luciano Bergamaschini* of Italy have been very valuable. The mind-expanding creativity of *Reijo Kääriäinen* has guided us to the very edges of human thinking. *Jaunita Brown's* forward thinking approach inspired us. Don Hoernig has worked with us from the very beginning.

Marshall Goldsmith and his team from Keilty, Goldsmith and Company have helped shape our thinking, particularly in the areas of measurement, feedback and follow-up.

A number of our associates sharpened our presentation.
We would like to thank the following people for taking time from their busy agendas to review our unedited manuscript and dialogue with us at length about changes and improvements: *Rick Canada* of Motorola; *John Lockitt* of Motorola Codex; *Larry Gibson* of Harvard Community Health Plan; *Dick Jelinek* of General Electric; *Dave Beard* of Northrop; *Jim Menoher* of Penn State Executive Programs; *Dan Welch* of Hill's Pet Nutrition/Colgate Palmolive; *Gustav Pansegrouw* from PE Corporate Services; *Howard Morgan* of Keilty, Goldsmith and Company; and *Chris Cappy* of Hollander, Kerrick and Cappy.

Our Via Team made special contributions.
A book is a perfect example of teamwork. *Cristine Ninteman* and *Virginia Kormanik* provided word processing support, *Pamela Taylor Waldman* assisted with graphics and layout and cover design, and *Carolyn Porte* and *Alan Gadney* of One on One provided editorial and printing assistance.

Kevin Liu, of our consulting team, was responsible for the integration and final articulation of many of the concepts in this book. He coordinated our production team, kept us on schedule, helped hone our ideas and provided substantial input and feedback to the content. His professional approach has been appreciated.

Finally, we would like to thank our children, Krista, Sophie, Tero Jr., Heather and Michael, and our extended families for their understanding and support.

February 1994
San Diego, California

Tero J. Kauppinen   Alexander J. Ogg, Jr.

PART ONE

TURBULENT TIMES

Chapter One

Turbulence: The White Water Decade

The people who change fastest and best are the ones who have no choice.

Robert Frey
Owner and President
The Cin-Made Corporation

As we all know, social change and advanced technology have caused the global business community to become increasingly fluid and turbulent in nature, like a stormy ocean or a succession of river rapids. The structure of business in this flowing and churning environment is apt to contain many surprises and dangers.

Challenges and opportunities may be right before us but we are not able to see them because we haven't the eyes to do so. And we no longer have the time nor the luxury to study, select options, and then implement our plans. Management of surprise has become the order of the day, and we must be ready to move as circumstances change. Timing business opportunities is very much like timing waves—a small misstep can drag you under or slap you against the side of the boat.

> ## Management of surprise has become
> ## the order of the day.

Like the sea, with its associated lack of stability—tides, waves, changeable weather, and powerful currents, the continuous variation of technology, customer whims, fashion, political correctness, communications capabilities, shareholder demands and employee concerns all require that we change assumptions and set different expectations than those that guided our decision-making—and profitability—in the past. Many mistakes have been made by managers who assumed that the business environment was more solid and stable than it actually is. That environment very often tossed them overboard.

Change drivers

When one can begin to think of and embrace the current business environment as a constantly moving fluid, one can also begin to understand why normal "change drivers"— global competition, customer sophistication, shareholder and employee expectations—become more influential within this metaphor. "Change drivers" are exactly what their name implies: factors that cause us to change our approach to business as they change. Imagine these change drivers as wind and current in our fluid environment. They may have very little impact on solid land, but out on the water their impact is quick and dramatic. Anyone who has been out to sea, or even on a weekend sail, will confirm this. A storm can hit without warning. We seek to turn change drivers into engines of opportunity.

Permanent white water

Peter Vaill, of George Washington University, termed the 90s the "Decade of *Permanent White Water*" (1989, italics ours). If the business environment has indeed become increasingly fluid, then Vaill's description is particularly apt. And anyone who has been white water rafting or kayaking—or is trying to be an excellent manager in today's world—can appreciate his metaphor.

Rowing on the River Thames

It is unfortunate, but most of our current organizations were designed during different times and for different environments. In the past, the operating environment was much "smoother" and more predictable. It was like a calm river or lake, with only mild breezes and ripples to contend with, and the game that was played was similar to the sport of crew. Organizations and their competitors functioned as crew teams, and everyone played by the same rules.

Crew members have very predictable roles, always sitting in the same seat in the shell and performing the same role in a predictable manner. Also, crew members must have similar physical assets: big biceps, large backs and strong thigh muscles. The manager (the coxswain—a "lightweight") sets the tempo, and the team creates the velocity. The shell is designed to move in a straight line and is very difficult to steer more than a few degrees to the right or left. The idea is to go as straight and as quick as possible. Pretty simple picture.

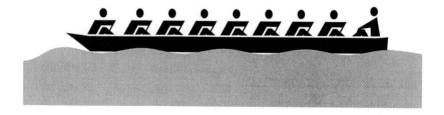

Figure 1: The Traditional Business Environment

Shooting the
Colorado River rapids

Now imagine taking the crew and shell down the Colorado River rapids. How ready is that team for this new environment? Their craft would probably be destroyed in seconds and the team members would be struggling on their own in some pretty dangerous white water.

How ready is your organization for the kind of rapid changes that are being caused by the *permanent white water* of the nineties?

Figure 2: Old Structure in the new Environment

Does your organization behave more like a crew shell or a rubber raft which was designed to be flexible and resilient in treacherous white water?

Figure 3: Adapting to the Environment

Our white water metaphor conjures up different kinds of basic work structures that will be effective in the coming years. There will be an unprecedented call and demand for flexible and creative leadership—similar to that of the experienced river guide who knows to run with the river, not against it. In addition, new kinds of workers will be needed to run these rapids—knowledgeable, adventurous, willing to take on the white water challenge, flexible enough to switch roles at a moment's notice. They will learn to expect new challenges and grow to love the exhilaration of change.

How ready is your organization for the *permanent white water* of the nineties?

Chapter Two

Measuring the Waves

An organizational transformation should be "launched as soon as the Capability Gap is diagnosed, without waiting for identification of the (organization's) future strategy."

Igor Ansoff (1993)

Measuring the waves

Igor Ansoff, the "Father of Strategic Management" can help us make some sense out of our chaotic business environment. He created a method to quantify the phenomenon on a standard scale and called it Environmental Turbulence (1979).

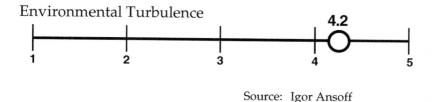

Environmental Turbulence

Source: Igor Ansoff

Figure 1: Assessing environmental turbulence

During the past several years we have asked managers who operate at various levels and work in a broad range of industries throughout the major world markets to rate the level of *Turbulence* in their operating environments. As you can see by the mark on the scale, an average of 4.2 on the 5 point scale, most view their environments as quite chaotic. They view their world as unusual, discontinuous and generally crazy and confusing. Many of the managers we work with have called it a world gone mad!

Take a moment to think about your own situation. Where on the scale would you rate the level of turbulence you face both professionally and personally?

The business response

If this is the general view, then the game has clearly changed from that of the past. However, the game must still be played. We cannot choose to stay home just because the water is too rough!

It is the *duty* of every strategic manager to help the organization win in this demanding environment. This requires the management team to craft a business response that will enable the organization to adapt and thrive in the midst of the chaos. Ideally, this business response would be a continuously perfect match with the ebbs, flows, and unexpectedness of the turbulence, rising and falling and take quick action appropriately as situations downstream are assessed.

Many management teams are struggling today as if they were that crew team caught in the rapids. Their past business response is no longer effective, and their traditional strategic management tools are worthless in a world gone mad. When we asked the same managers mentioned in the previous section about their business response in relation to the level of environmental turbulence they experienced, most indicated that they lagged behind the demands of the situation. They were trying to turn the boat after it had already struck the rocks. To use another metaphor, the hunters were trying to shoot the duck by aiming *behind* the bird. Many managers expressed significant frustration in "playing catch-up," and reacting to the competition, rather than being ahead and anticipating.

The scales depicted below, Business Response ("strategic response" in Ansoff's original work) on Environmental Turbulence, show how one relates to the other. Managers describe that on average, in the environmental storm of 4.2, their organization's business response has been 3.4.

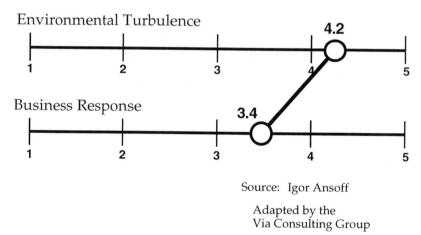

Source: Igor Ansoff

Adapted by the
Via Consulting Group

*Figure 2: Business response compared
to environmental turbulence*

Organizational readiness

A third scale is needed to complete the current business picture. Strategic managers have traditionally attempted to craft a business response that is sufficiently aggressive to address the demands of their environments. The tools utilized have been vision (meaning and fulfillment), mission (setting direction and boundaries) and strategy (enablers).

Many organizations have spent hours of executive time and thousands of consulting dollars to select and define this current business response, only to *fail in implementation.*

> ## Implementation has been characterized as "the management challenge of the nineties."

This failure may be shown by utilizing a third scale. The addition of organizational readiness ("managerial capability" in Ansoff's original work) to implement the business response completes the picture, indicating the true depth of the problem. Managers rate the readiness of their organizations an average of 1.4 to 2.8 points behind the turbulence level of the environment. The organization is trying to ride the white water without a craft or means of steerage, unable to see what lies ahead, desperately slow in reacting to situations as they arise, and making some progress, but being battered to death in the process. To use our hunting metaphor, not only are the hunters aiming behind the duck, but the gun is jammed, and birds are whizzing by, one after another, while the chamber is being cleared! One missed opportunity after another.

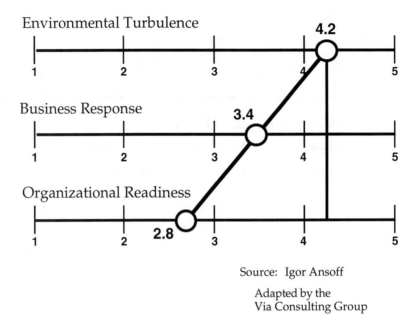

Source: Igor Ansoff

Adapted by the
Via Consulting Group

*Figure 3:   Organizational readiness compared
to the business response*

Some of Igor Ansoff's most recent findings
(1993, pp. 19, 20-21, 28) indicate that:

1)   A strategic gap of 1.5 to 2 points between
environmental turbulence and organizational
readiness translates to a drop in organizational
performance to near 0.

2)   Strategic responsiveness—readiness for change—
is the key success variable in highly turbulent
environments.

3)   The more dependent an organization is on its
environment—the more reactive it is as opposed
to proactive—the more poorly it performs.

Chapter Three

Creating Renewable Competitive Advantage

Leaders are prepared to sacrifice the easy life for difficulty, and, ultimately, sustained competitive advantage.

Michael Porter

The reactive zone—
doing things *better*

Organizations that have been able to discover the fundamental problem of lagging organizational readiness and inadequate business response are beating their competition either in strategy or implementation. Their competitive advantage over the last decade has been the result of crafting and implementing initiatives that have created "purposeful motion" along the Organizational Readiness continuum. The term "purposeful motion" was coined by Paul Galvin of Motorola. "Purposeful motion" may be defined as those decisions and actions that drive an organization toward an anticipated and planned-for future. By engaging in purposeful motion, competitors have been able to consistently differentiate themselves from their competitors in the eyes of their customers and shareholders—and have been rewarded accordingly. Some of the successful initiatives: Total Quality Management, Restructuring, Right-sizing, Cost-cutting, Cycle Time Improvements, Process Improvements, etc. The list goes on.

> **"Purposeful motion" may be defined as those decisions and actions that drive an organization toward an anticipated and planned-for future.**

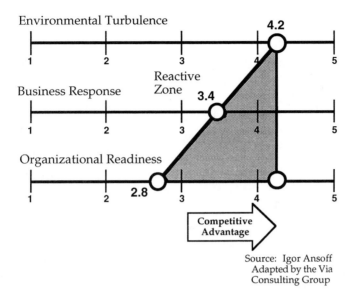

Figure 1: The area of reactive strategies

Returning to our graphical representation, one can see that the arrow along the continuum has indeed produced some competitive advantage and created turbulence for those less ready for change. This is purposeful motion. Notable examples of riding the waves in this "reactive zone" are General Electric in the strategy arena and the Chrysler of the 80s in the implementation arena.

Competitive advantage has definitely come to those organizations that have been able to *do things better*. This continuous improvement mindset and related behaviors have created some excellent process companies that truly can continuously improve. However, although continuous improvement is necessary for competitive advantage, it is not sufficient to produce *renewable* competitive advantage. Incremental and evolutionary change will not meet the demands of a revolutionary environment. In other words, better paddles cannot compare to a jet boat for traversing the river. A single technological innovation can change the game so dramatically that you can literally be out of the game no matter how good your existing offerings may be.

If this is the case, how can renewable competitive advantage be produced in a permanent white water environment?

Creating turbulence in the proactive zone— Doing things *differently*

In order to thrive during these times of chaos, a change in mindset—a new paradigm—is needed. It is not enough to continuously improve or keep pace with the environment. We have to get out and aim ahead of the duck! We have to anticipate! And, in doing so, *we will create turbulence* for our competitors.

This calls for a completely different way of thinking and acting. It is not simply doing things better, it is doing things *differently*. And not different for difference's sake. The shift in paradigm is necessary for survival in the future, but it also means a renewal at the center of the organization. It means creating an organization that is constantly ready for change. It means innovating, creating and learning in fundamentally new ways that can change your organization and change the face of business as well.

This new paradigm is graphically represented by creating an proactive zone overlay on the three same descriptive scales:

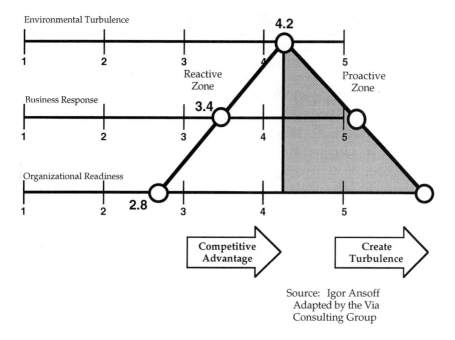

Figure 2: The area of proactive strategies

Alternatively, the situation can be viewed in another way if three different approaches to competition are considered and created on a chart like the next one:

TRADITIONAL COMPETITION	COMPETITIVE ADVANTAGE	"SUSTAINABLE" COMPETITIVE ADVANTAGE
• Make the sale • Increase volume • Standard Products Menu • Respond to Customer Requests • Competitive prices, quality, service and delivery as compared to the market	• Broaden product line purchases • Secure long-term contracts • Make them product/technology dependent • Get design-in wins • Superb service • On-time delivery • Volume-based competitive pricing	• Customer is more important than the sale • Ensure the customer's success first • Understand their business better than they do • Provide solutions to problems • Anticipate their needs • Develop fully trusted partnerships • Value-based pricing • Eliminate service requirement

Table 1: Changing nature of competitive advantage.
Developed by David Pulatie, Motorola Inc.

Competition—
The traditional approach

Competition in the past was defeated by better products, lower costs, superior service, higher quality or a combination thereof. The game was still the same, the rules were unvarying and well-known, and the next year's strategic plan was based on the past year's performance in relation to those factors as they affected market share.

Building competitive advantage— *The Terminator*

During the mid-1980s, *The Terminator (1984)*, starring famous body-builder and actor Arnold Schwarzenegger, was a box office hit. As a nearly unbeatable foe that had significant advantage in combat, *The Terminator* provides us with an interesting management metaphor. Although his technological advancements enabled him to battle beyond our normal expectations, he still fought with the same weapons and in the same way. And ultimately his mechanical advantages met a mechanical end.

Adaptive initiatives like total quality, cycle time improvements and restructuring, can help improve organizational processes to the point that we can produce "Terminator-like" businesses, seemingly invincible leviathans that consume increasing market share—until someone changes the game and introduces *Terminator II: Judgment Day...*

Renewable competitive advantage— Creating turbulence with *Terminator II*

Terminator II: Judgment Day (1991) also starred Schwarzenegger as the Terminator, but he was obsolete compared to the T9000, an opponent with a superior flexible and resilient structure that could learn instantaneously, adapt chameleon-like to its environment, and battle in completely unconventional and unexpected ways. There was no way of anticipating its responses to situations because machinery that could behave like a fluid was outside the "normal" mechanical realm. Able to pass through jail bars, melt unnoticed into the floor or instantly reassemble itself into different configurations, it appeared invincible. Ultimately, only luck and human determination caused its demise.

This Terminator/Terminator II story offers some interesting insights that can be applied to organizational survival. Renewable advantage will be built by those organizations that can begin to act like the T9000, learning instantaneously, adapting to and flowing with the demands of an increasingly turbulent environment.

However, we are not advocating one model or approach over another. The key is to diagnose where on the turbulence scale your business currently operates and then act accordingly to design initiatives and approaches that will create the competitive advantage to satisfy customers, employees and shareholders.

From long range planning to strategic management

Management systems have been evolving over the past 40 years in response to relatively incremental changes in the environment.

Long Range Planning became very popular following World War II. Planning and management systems were designed to respond to a stable growth marketplace. This was essentially rear view mirror management in which the current year's operating plan was created by reviewing last year's results and penciling in the projected or desired sales increases. Performance management consisted of photocopying last year's goals with this year's date. Management by Objectives systems were created during this period, and worked well until the business environment began to shift.

Strategic Planning was initiated by the oil crisis of the early seventies. The inability of management systems to anticipate this kind of startling and discontinuous change caused a reassessment of the way companies were managed, leading to the birth of strategic planning. This system created individual planning departments, but it was typical for strategic planning efforts to be frustrated by line executives who would challenge the validity of new information and make "gut" decisions based on their experiences and perceptions. While this was fine at one time, it has become increasingly ineffective as the operating environment is less and less a reflection of the past. In addition, planning departments are frequently plagued by "analysis paralysis," and by the time the situation has been studied and a recommendation has been made, circumstances have changed and the data is longer valid or useful.

Strategic management has supplanted strategic planning as the most pervasive approach to managing an organization.

Pioneered by such innovators as Igor Ansoff, the basic approach is one of having line managers take responsibility and an active role in determining the strategic direction of the organization. Rather than having an analysis conducted by a planning function, affected managers would engage in: 1) studying the environment; 2) devising the strategic response that would meet the demands of that environment; and 3) implementing the strategy that would match the present capabilities of the organization with environmental opportunities and ensuring the development of future capabilities.

Most effective organizations have some sort of strategic management process that has been adopted by their executive teams. Unfortunately, these systems are already obsolete and inadequate when faced with the turbulence of the current decade. As we will see, organizations in the hottest industry segments are reinventing the art of strategic management faster than the academics can document or the consultants can help.

> **Renewable advantage will be built by those organizations that can learn instantaneously, and adapt to and flow with the demands of an increasingly turbulent environment.**

New *strategic leadership* is needed.

The New Strategic Leadership— Turning the organization into a learning machine

As we have said, the reality of today's business environment is that it has become increasingly turbulent. Turbulence brings disequilibrium, novelty, loss of control and surprise. These were not the watch words of the manager of the past because most conventional wisdom said to avoid surprise and loss of control at all costs.

The search for organizational equilibrium is the sure path to institutional death. Organizations are open systems that must engage with their environment and continue to grow and evolve or they will die. Margaret Wheatley in her innovative book, *Leadership and the New Science*, (1993), states that "open systems have the possibility to continuously import free energy from the environment and of exporting entropy." This means that entropy—which is the tendency for closed systems, like machines, to gradually breakdown and disintegrate—can become the "exhaust" of organizational renewal!

It is therefore necessary to ensure that your organization is linked with its customers in such a way as to remain an open system and not fall prey to the success dialectic. The success dialectic was articulated by George Fisher, former CEO of Motorola and currently CEO of Kodak. He warned that too often, "Success, breeds arrogance...arrogance causes us to stop listening to our Key Publics (customers)…and this leads to decline." When an open system starts to become closed, entropy sets in and then it is only a matter of time before decline leads to a slow and painful death.

> **"Success, breeds arrogance…**
> **arrogance causes us**
> **to stop listening to our key publics…**
> **and this leads to decline."**
> **George Fisher, CEO, Kodak**

Creating organizational disequilibrium— Learning and renewal

Wheatley goes on to say, "To stay viable, open systems must maintain a state of disequilibrium, keeping the system off balance so that it can change and grow." Organizations have used quarterly review processes as a negative feedback system to monitor results and maintain stability. Regulatory or negative feedback loops served this function well, signaling any departures from the norm. As managers watched for sub-standard performance, they could make corrections and preserve the system.

But there are new types of feedback loops—positive ones that *amplify responses and phenomena*. These loops use information differently, not to regulate but to *amplify* troublesome messages. In these loops, *information increases and disturbances grow*. The current negative feedback system, unable to deal with so much magnifying information, is being asked to change. For those interested in system stability, amplification is very threatening and there is an attempt to quell it. "This new initiative is like a small nuclear device, ready to explode in our organization..." stated a senior executive when looking at the disequilibrium being caused by a new strategic initiative.

Interest has turned from system structures to system dynamics as the environment has become more fluid. Successful organizations have learned that "purposeful disturbances" create disequilibrium, and that this very same disequilibrium can lead to growth. This is scary for traditional managers who have spent their careers monitoring and controlling.

Disequilibrium is unpredictable. If you talk to a "change-wise" senior executive, she will tell you that these new initiatives are always scary, that there is no controlling them and that you are never sure where they are going to go. But they almost always lead to positive change for the organization. Change is not a fearsome opponent. The leaders of the future will create new relationships with change and disorder.

> **Purposeful disturbances create**
> **disequilibrium that leads to growth.**

Positive feedback loops create disturbances and disequilibrium

Faced with amplifying levels of disturbance, the new systems possess innate properties to reconfigure themselves so that they can deal with the new information. For this reason they are frequently called self-organizing or self-renewing systems. One of their distinguishing features is system resiliency as opposed to system rigidity.

Part of their viability comes from their internal capacity to create structures that fit the moment. Neither form nor function alone dictate how the system is constructed. Instead, form and function engage in a fluid process where the system may maintain itself in its present form or evolve to a new order. The system possesses the capacity for spontaneously emerging structures. When the needs change, so does the organizational structure. But an organization can only exist in such fluid fashion if it has access to new information, both from external and internal sources.

Environmental and internal information must be feed renewal

Openness to environmental information over time spawns a firmer sense of identity, one that is less permeable to externally-induced change. A business that focuses on its core competencies identifies itself as a portfolio of capabilities rather than a portfolio of business units. For example, Sony effectively leveraged its core capability of miniaturization. Rather than diversifying its portfolio of businesses, it leveraged its technical platforms, such as the Walkman, of which there are now more than 200 versions.

Many companies have learned the hard way that diversifying in areas in which they have no core competency is risky. Volvo paid a high price for this lesson after venturing into the oil business. On the surface, this seemed logically linked to the auto industry, but in reality, totally different capabilities were demanded.

An organization that is focused on core competencies is both sensitive to its environment and yet resistant to its influences. In this way it is wide open to new opportunities and ventures that welcome its particular skills. Companies focused on core competencies are able to "invent new markets, quickly enter emerging markets and drastically shift patterns of customer choice in established markets" (Pralahad and Hamel, 1991).

Most executives we know agree with these ideas. But their immediate questions always are, "How do you make all this practical? What are some of the proven methods that will make this work?

The Change Engine

In order to respond to that request we have developed the Change Engine to create continuous organizational change and adaptation. The example pictured below has the following features:

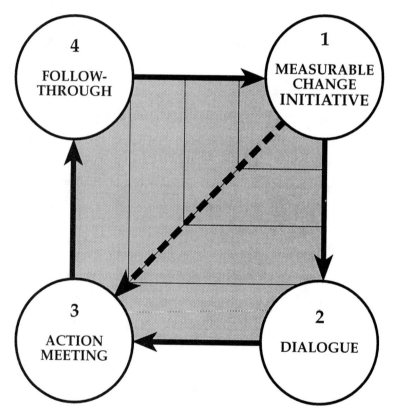

Figure: 3 The Change Engine

- It represents a new management system for the turbulent times in the future. It will replace the worn out management systems of the past.

- It contains a double-loop for the identification and resolution of local and organizational errors (Argyris, 1982).

- It promotes continuous organizational learning and change (Senge, 1990).

- It puts the organization into disequilibrium— "purposeful motion" allowing it to become self-renewing and resilient (Galvin, Motorola, Inc. and Wheatley, 1993).

- It promotes horizontal integration of organizational "silos" thereby reducing horizontal violence. This "small within large" methodology allows for seamless integration, boundarylessness and border-lessness. (Canavan, Motorola, Inc. and Welch, General Electric).

- Finally, it integrates the "best of the best" proven change methodologies that have withstood the test of practicality in innovative organizations like Ford and Xerox.

Change engines work like oil pumps pumping crude issues for the organization to refine into action. The change engines work while the leader is away; they are subsystems that a leader puts in place to pump energy for the change and create continuous transformation.

What does
it take to change?

Organizations compete on their *ability to convert information into timely action.* Change involves doing that more effectively. Mark B. Fuller used Pentagon sources to illustrate this point in his article in *Fast Company Journal,* October 1993:

Gather better information...that is, information that is dynamic, that cuts across organizational boundaries, and that exists in real time.

Establish a framework for making decisions... that is, create a business version of military doctrine that provides integration between ends and means.

Practice the integration of the pieces...that is, learn to see details, problems and challenges in their context and understand the situation more holistically.

These three categories seem to be relevant to managing change. If a leader has real time information, which can be processed through a reliable and valid framework so that everybody can understand the pieces in their context, the probability of success is fairly high. One can see this even more clearly, if the opposite picture is painted. What would be the probability of success if a leader made changes based on inaccurate, old information, without understanding how the pieces influence and relate to each other, and the team felt confused about the change?

The quest for
a new approach

When engaging leaders in discussion about their worries and concerns, one can clearly hear the reasons for organizational failure:

> *"We know what needs to happen.*
> *But we never implement. Action just does not happen."*

> *"We are so damned slow!*
> *By the time we pull the trigger, the target has moved."*

> *"Our information is in the wrong place at the wrong time."*

> *"Vision is great, but our goals never get implemented."*

> *"The last thing we need is a vision.*
> *We have some real work to do."*

> *"How can you expect strategies to be put into action, when*
> *even the executives aren't fully committed to them?"*

Maybe the most revealing comment was from an executive who expressed his frustration at his organization's inability to change by saying,

> *"We are going to hell—in First Class!"*

For some companies, the list of implementation problems includes intense internal competition escalated into turf wars, silo effects and resource struggles between units. The traditional approaches to change often seem to nurture individual competition rather than cooperation. A new approach is needed.

PART TWO

THE LEADER'S GUIDE

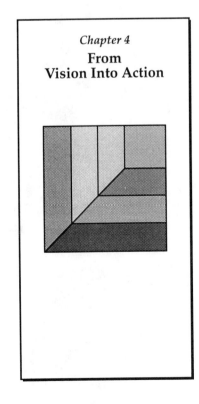

Chapter 4
**From
Vision Into Action**

Chapter Four

From Vision Into Action

What makes a transformational leader's job so difficult is the dynamic and complex nature of organizations.

Noel Tichy

The quantum leap within leadership

Earth shaking changes in the business environment demand organizational responses equal to the strategic and operational challenge. Strategy development and implementation will have to become simultaneous. Planners and implementers must begin to work as a single entity. Organizations must learn to become "small within large" as a matter of survival—maintaining the resource strengths of a large corporation while attaining the speed and maneuverability of smaller companies. Business and people issues must be processed holistically, not piecemeal, as in the past.

All of these changes mean that roles and functions are changing too. Human resource professionals, while once the organization's "administrators of mercy and justice," are fast becoming key facilitators of change. No longer simply managers of the personnel function, human resource professionals are coordinating major organizational transitions, counseling senior management about the implications of a change process, and in many instances, providing key input to the transformation architecture.

The last vestiges of the old, tired and fragmented Weberian bureaucracy are being welded into a seamless customer-driven network by the people closest to the action—salespersons and all others having first-hand experience with customers.

A turbulent business environment is only a reflection of equivalent tumult in larger society. As the pace of change constantly increases, driven by technological advances, political turmoil and social upheaval, the very nature of "work" and of the people who do it—is changing.

The changing nature of work

It is now quite common for leaders to be managing teams and virtual organizations composed of members from numerous constituencies including vendors, client or supplier organizations, distributors and other strategic partners. The power base for leading such teams is vastly different from the simple command and control of the past.

Accountability and responsibility are changing shape as individuals become members of more than one team. Traditional leadership styles accounted for only one role to be filled by each direct report. The locus of control is moving from within the leader to within the follower.

Increased access to information on a real-time basis is also decreasing the effectiveness of old leadership structures. Organizational members are now privy to much information that, in the past, was strictly the domain of management. Leaders are no longer *the* source of information.

The changing nature of the workforce

Much has been written about increasing diversity in the workforce, and leaders must become expert at managing the variety of diverse ethnicity's, nationalities, preferences and differences that make up today's workforce. As minorities become the majority, and a variety of languages, cultures, beliefs and habits enter into the organizational mix, employees can no longer be managed as a uniform and stereotypical whole, but must be led as individuals, each having a unique combination of history, experience, culture and competencies.

This trend towards individual acknowledgment and acceptance is not solely a function of the "shrinking global village." It is a generational difference as well. "Baby busters," "Generation X," the "13ers," whichever designation one chooses for those born between 1961 and 1981, are, as a cohort, much more self aware than generations past, and, because of the turbulence of the times, exhibit a more intense search for *meaning and purpose*. Even those in the previous "baby boomer" generation also desire to seek new levels of purpose, as the concern and anxiety over competitive advantage, downsizing, middle aged incompetence, and growing social anarchy has affected them as well. *These people are all beginning to look for purpose and meaning in their work*, as well as in their extracurricular activities—something in line with their values and something larger than their individual, daily responsibilities. Increasingly, they are no longer willing to simply fulfill a function—regardless of potential monetary return. This search for purpose and meaning requires that leaders acquire skills that go beyond the scope of typical organizational and individual leadership. Abraham Zeleznik (1977) has proposed that managers are concerned about how things get done while leaders are concerned with what things mean to people. This emphasis on the need for meaning is addressed in the next chapter.

How leaders lead—
what have we learned about leadership

Leadership theories, and research and publications about those theories, abound. Every academic article one reads about leadership begins with such statements, most of them quoting Stogdill's (1974) conclusion that, "there are almost as many definitions of leadership as there are persons who have attempted to define the concept." Articles in the popular press, while avoiding the controversies of definition and "best" leadership approaches, tend to be cyclical in nature, skimming off the tops of whatever current leadership models or theories are in vogue.

As stated in our previous chapters, we have entered a time in which all of our old models and paradigms are less valid and useful. Gary Yukl, in 1989, stated that, "The field of leadership is presently in a state of ferment and confusion. Most of the theories are beset with conceptual weaknesses and lack strong empirical support." Apparently, this knowledge is not recent as this concern has been evident throughout the study of leadership. Stogdill confirmed this in 1974, concluding that, "Four decades of research on leadership have produced a bewildering mass of findings…"

We must cull from the past those aspects of leadership practice that will continue to be useful in the future and blend them together into a working model that is sufficiently flexible to address all eventualities as they evolve. It's a tall order. The emphasis here is on a *working* model, not an academic theory; on practice, not research.

Let's first begin with a *very* brief overview of major leader-ship approaches from the past, in order to determine what is useful and what is not.

Trait approach

The trait approach to leadership reverts to the 1930s and 1940s during which hundreds of trait studies were con-ducted to discover the elusive qualities of the "Great Man." Research at that time focused primarily on personality traits and general intelligence. More recently, the trait approach has focused on specific skill sets and personal motivation factors.

Power-influence approach

This approach, as its name implies, is centered on the types and amounts of power and influence that a leader exercises. French and Raven's (1959) typology has been widely accepted for years. A variety of influence tactics have been investigated, including benefit exchange, pressure tactics, appeal to authority, rational persuasion, consultation, and inspirational appeal.

The recent emphasis on *charismatic power* is strongly related to the power-influence approach as well as the trait approach, and is indicative of an increased search for answers to leadership issues in an uncertain time.

Behavioral approach

Behavioral researchers have emphasized those activities in which leaders actually engage to increase their effectiveness. It is within this approach that all of the controversy over leadership vs. management resides. Many of the studies have emphasized the two-factor conception of leadership that includes task-oriented behaviors and relationship-oriented behaviors, and utilize the Ohio State leadership scales (Fleishman, 1953).

Participative leadership, with the emphasis on empowerment and delegation, also comes under the behavioral approach and has received increased attention in recent times. Although 35 years of research have been inconclusive, numerous case studies of effective managers seem to support participative leadership as an effective tool during changing times.

Situational approach

The situational approach includes many of the models currently in use today. Common to all is the adaptive use of different leadership strategies appropriate for a particular follower's willingness and abilities.

What has been confusing is the degree to which leadership behavior and situational variables influence one another. There are a number of familiar models, including Path-Goal Theory (Evans, 1970), Fiedler's Contingency Theory (1967), Vroom and Yetton's Normative Decision Theory (1973), LMX Theory (Dansereau, Graen, & Haga, 1975), and

Situational Leadership Theory (Hersey & Blanchard, 1969). Today's leaders require an intuitive and simple model to apply to their ever-changing situations, almost an adjustable template that can be tailored to meet each new requirement. The originators of the various situational approaches have greatly contributed to this model.

Transformational approaches

Transformational leadership has come to the forefront in recent years as an approach to addressing internal motivation. Where previously addressed approaches influence external motivators, more turbulent times have called for this somewhat different approach. Transformational leadership is more broadly defined than those models previously discussed and includes aspects of trait, power, behavioral and situational models. As such, it can provide some parts of the more all-encompassing, practical model that we are seeking.

Transformational leadership emphasizes complete shifts in organizational culture and changes in the perception of the business environment, and became increasingly prevalent during the late 1980s and early 1990s. A response to environmental threats from foreign and domestic competition, increasing customer demand and revolutionary changes in technology, transformational leadership places emphasis on process, such as empowerment and delegation in order to achieve major changes in culture and strategy. It contrasts with other approaches in that it contains a more philosophical bent, creating new dimensions to consider. With increased emphasis on creativity and innovation as competitive advantage, this approach has merit, utilizing inspiration and vision as motivators.

Charismatic leadership, a more narrowly defined concept, refers to followers' perceptions of a leader as possessing almost superhuman qualities. Leader influence and power, therefore, are more an issue of personal persuasion of individuals than of an interactive process. The charismatic approach is somewhat similar to the old "Great Man" model of the 1940s trait theories.

The current fascination with the charismatic approach poses both opportunity and threat to organizational leadership. On the one hand, the desire for strong, visionary, larger-than-life leadership is indicative of the leadership vacuum that currently exists and of followers' desires to have their fears and anxieties about the future alleviated. On the other hand, the very fact that followers' may seek such unrealistic leadership figures poses a significant challenge to enabling them to perceive the realities of change and the need to address their own personal apprehensions.

The Via Model

After reviewing the multitude of leadership theories, that have been generated over the last sixty years, it is obvious that no single approach has been sufficient, there is no "one best way." Clearly, different levels of change require entirely different models and approaches. Within a single organization, both transactional and transformational leadership styles will be necessary. Both the future and the past must be addressed. We have culled the "best of the best" to form the Via Model.

The Via Model combines "the best of the best."

If we slice an organization like an onion, we get a picture of how things are structured, from the broad key players level (customers, suppliers, etc.) down to each individual within the company.

Figure 1: The "onion cut" of an organization

However, it is quite obvious from this next figure that the interplay between the human and business elements of the organization is quite confusing and messy, with overlapping layers and hidden pieces. Unlike the ubiquitous organizational chart, this meshing of elements is an organizational reality.

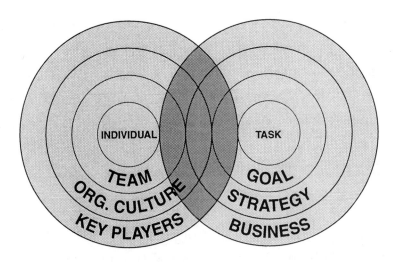

*Figure 2: Matching the layers of leadership and
management processes in an organization*

If vision is the picture of the preferred future on the mission
road to success, then the Via, Vision Into Action Model provides the *holistic framework* for making sense of the elements
pictured above and organizing them for effective executive
decision-making and leadership.

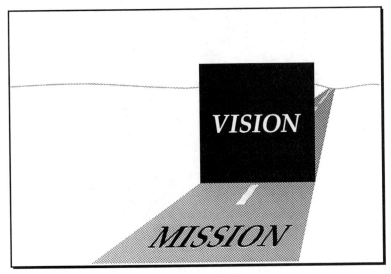

Figure 3: Vision picture on the mission road

The Model serves as a *diagnostic paradigm* by which one can collect fragmented information, put it into context and understand it in a new, more comprehensive way. It covers all aspects, from creating direction for an organization to determining the tasks of an individual. It *maps out interrelationships* and offers a practical solution for leaders to deal effectively with the complexities of change.

Via provides a model for true leadership—to understand and utilize transformational (organizational), transactional (between individuals), and personal (within an individual) leadership interventions at appropriate organizational levels. The goal is to design structures and processes that function to create *virtual perfection* between the survival needs of the organization and the personal needs of its people.

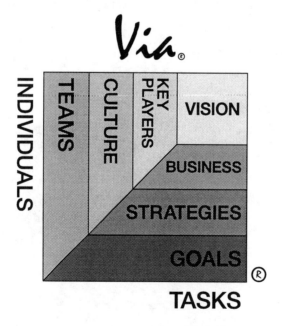

Figure 4: The Via Model

Originally, the Via Model emerged from the shared pain of a client and consultant, when old approaches no longer produced desired results and a more holistic solution was needed. When the focus was primarily on changing business elements, such as divisional goals or long-term strategies, the "people" side of the business was ignored which greatly hampered implementation. If we turned our attention to the organizational culture and individuals, without attending to business elements, no one was piloting the ship. Addressing only one side or the other didn't work.

The missing link that triggered the development of the model was information about the human brain. After all, decisions result from a process which occurs in the brain. The knowledge of brain physiology and the primary functions of different lobes, led to an evaluation of the processes that occur in organizations when decisions and changes take place; when goals and emotions, strategies and culture, people and business simultaneously influence human thought and behavior.

The Via Model consists of two axes, anchored by the concept of vision. The right axis contains future-oriented business elements, while the left axis brings people elements into the model; their skills, abilities, perceptions, concerns, and collective history.

While many models of organizational change emphasize either the business or the people elements of an organization, Via provides a holistic picture that allows accurate diagnosis.

By viewing the organization through this framework, a leader can determine if the business idea is acceptable to its key players, if proposed strategies are consistent with the organization's culture, if established goals can actually be implemented by the teams for which they were created, or if individuals have the skills and/or willingness to carry out their tasks.   In addition, the model assists in defining whether the problem is one of attunement—people and historical issues, or alignment—business and futures issues.

Business life cycles and the Via Model

"Business ideas" define an organization's key business essentials, including its target market, products and services, and resources and systems. They have a life span or cycle that is dependent upon the operating environment, technological advances, customer preference and need, and company direction. In order to remain competitive, new business ideas must be created even as the old ones are waning.

This transition from old to new is often accompanied by turbulence within the company, caused by product loyalty, ego, fear of the unknown future, lack of confidence or a host of other reasons. The future and the past collide. However, to stay in the game, each organization must cross the turbulence from maintenance of the old idea to the transformation associated with the new.

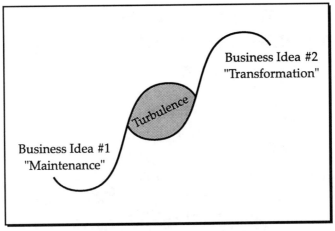

Figure 5: Organizational renewal—
putting turbulence in a business context

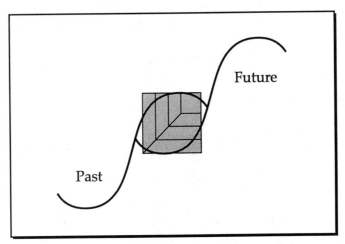

Figure 6: Managing the turbulence of the
business transformation using the Via Model.
Developed with Rick Canada, Motorola, Inc.

The Via Model assists in managing the turbulence of a business transformation by combining the people with the business—the past with the future—on an easily diagnosed template.

Alignment: the business management process

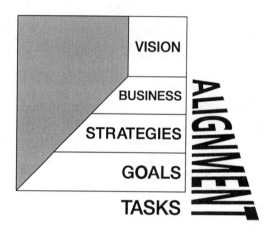

Figure 7: Alignment in the Via Model

The right axis of the Via Model transitions from task to organizational vision. The tasks you carry out should be in line with your goals. These personal and team goals should support strategies, which in turn should lead to achieving business objectives and overall organizational vision. If different levels of the process are supporting each other in this way, an organization is said to be *aligned*.

Alignment can be an important issue *within* the right axis of the model. Business objectives should be aligned with each other. Misalignment between business objectives may occur, but it is far more common on the strategic or goal levels; strategies should be aligned with each other and with the structures to achieve them; goals should be similarly aligned with each other and with internal systems as well.

The Via Model without people: Only half a story

The alignment process is important, but represents only half of the management and leadership process, often the easier part. If alignment issues were the only things which leaders had to address, managers could fulfill their roles and expectations simply through planning and execution.

People make a plan live and breathe. At the same time, they make a manager's work more challenging.

As previously mentioned, the left side of the Via Model represents an organization's collective past. People bring to a situation their knowledge, experiences, skills, beliefs, attitudes and more. When people's future seems like it will be similar to their past, they most naturally move towards their preferred future. But since change has become so rapid and has created unexpected results a "natural" gap opens between the comfortable past and the preferred future. This gap forms the leadership challenge for which the Via Model was developed.

People and the VIA Model— Attunement: the leadership process

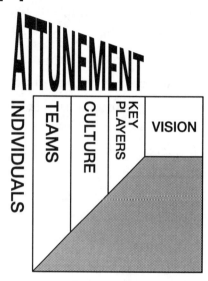

Figure 8: Attunement in the Via Model

Attunement occurs when each of the levels on the left side of the model support one another; when individuals have their own visions in mind and can support their teams, when the teams and the organizational culture are consistent, and when the culture of the institution accommodates all of the key players. Attunement is a concept often neglected in change efforts, yet it has a very strong influence on the success of the change.

The figure below graphically represents an organization out of alignment and attunement. It is easy to imagine what this might look like in real life.

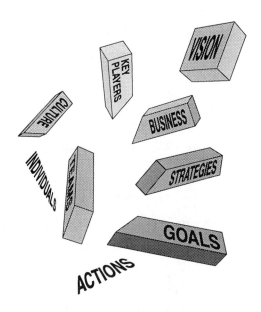

Figure 9: An organization out of alignment and attunement.

The first four chapters have shown the practical gap that exists between the people and business sides of an organization.

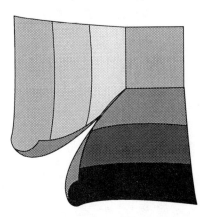

*Figure 10: The gap between the people
and business sides of an organization*

The next five chapters will close that gap and address the different levels of change that occur in an organization. As a three dimensional construct, the Via Model addresses these matches between the human and business axes that can lead to organizational success. Each level has its own issues and "change triggers" that can facilitate the change process. We speak of "matches" within the model because change is best accomplished when there is consistency between the business and its key players, between organizational culture and strategies, between teams and their goals, and between individuals and the tasks for which they are responsible.

We hope that these last chapters will provide the reader with a practical overview of the different levels of change within an organization. Each section may be read on its own as a primer to achieving change within the company or within oneself.

PART THREE

DRIVING CHANGE

VISIONARY LEVEL
Chapter 5 **Creating the Future** *Chapter 6* **Visionary Leadership**

↓

STRATEGIC LEVEL
Chapter 7 **Strategic Leadership:** **The Change Engines**

↓

TEAM LEVEL
Chapter 8 **Team Leadership:** **Making It Work**

↓

INDIVIDUAL LEVEL
Chapter 9 **Personal Transformation:** **Via My Way**

Chapter Five

Creating the Future

*Where there is no vision,
the people perish.*

Proverbs 29:18

Establishing the purpose

Defining mission is the most fundamental action an organization will take. The mission statement describes the reason for existence. No theories or models can assist an organization that no longer has a valid reason for existence. Many failed organizations defined their reason for being in internal terms and based on internal needs. For example, the purpose of a company is not to "make money" for the organization or its owners. Financial rewards are the consequence of being effective in implementing the mission.

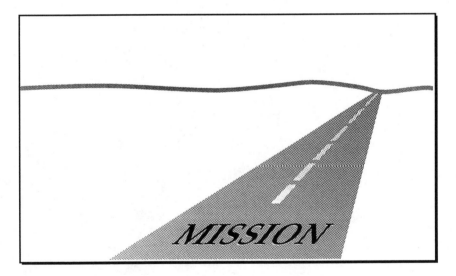

Figure 1: Mission is the selected road to success

Purpose may be found outside of the organization, by serving customers and satisfying their needs. A good mission statement is *expressed in customer-driven terms.*

"We are improving the effectiveness of the retail industry through customized store equipment and solutions."

—Pan-Oston, Inc.

Pan-Oston, Inc. is a European family business that, in only a few short years, has grown into the market leader in the North American retail check-out counter business.

Failure in defining mission

According to the International Management and Leadership Survey (LSI, 1992), nearly 100 percent of executives agree that defining mission is important for an organization. Most of the organizations have a definite mission, but only about 75 percent of them really use their mission statements in the planning process.

When asked what was behind this survey result, most leaders thought that their mission statement was more for the annual report or for PR use than for guiding their planning or decision making processes. During recessionary times, leaders were fighting for survival and the guiding "mission" seemed to be one of "making the quarterly quota." This short-term focus often led to detrimental decisions for the longer-term.

If a mission statement is not defined with the customer in mind, its definition can easily become production-oriented or inward-directed. We might think that we are "building

the best railway engines in the world" or "we're in the railway business," when, in actuality, we are part of the transportation business. In failing to clearly see the organizational purpose, a company can make a fatal error in creating
too narrow or short-sighted a definition for its mission.

On the other hand, an organization can state its mission so
broadly that it might be labeled "one-size-fits-all." In this case,
the mission is so general that it does not have the power to
steer the organization or differentiate it from any others.

> ## "We are helping our customers
> ## achieve better results."

This mission could belong to a financial corporation, a law
firm, a printing company, a transportation company, a
training company, an advertising agency, or an accounting
practice. Equally, any competitor of these different companies could choose exactly the same mission.

Figure 2: Defining the edges of the Mission Statement

A good mission is customer oriented. It must be simultaneously broad enough and narrow enough to provide direction
for organizational decision-making while providing a platform for definition of the organization's vision.

Vision describes
your preferred future

Vision is the mirror image of one's internal and fundamental
core beliefs. However, the terms mission and vision are often used interchangeably. Consequently, their definitions
have blurred, and each one lacks crispness and clarity. For
that reason we need to define the terms for our discussion.

Earlier we defined mission as *the road to success*. Out of all
the many roads, you have made a single choice. The decision can be illustrated as choice "C" in Figure 3.

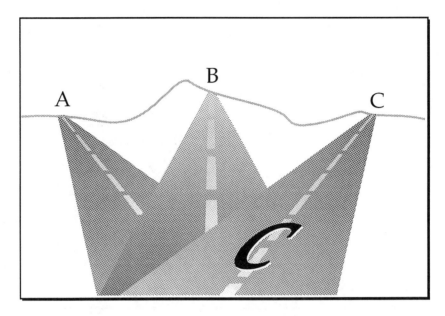

Figure 3: Choices for your mission, the road to success

When you have made your choice, say, chosen the road "C" in the figure, it is then possible to define vision.

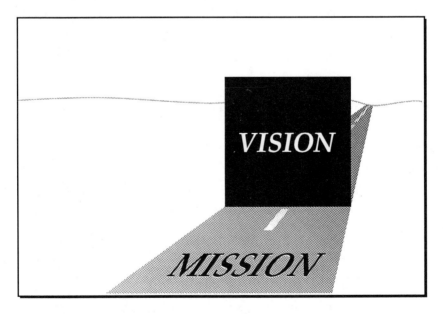

Figure 4: The relationship of vision and mission

Vision is the picture of the preferred future at a given point
in time. By emphasizing different aspects of vision, we can
define it in several ways:

Vision is a definition of our success... We paint our future
on the billboard of our mission road by defining what our
success looks like at a given point in time in the future.

Vision is a mental picture... As such, the clearer the picture,
the more programming power the vision has in our minds.
A picture not clearly seen, cannot strongly influence our actions. Too often, vision is only a set of statements that sound
good, but do not become vivid pictures in people's minds.

Vision is value-anchored will... Vision is a declaration of
organizational will, or the will of a particular team or individual. It reflects the inner values of an entity. A good vision has its root deep in people's minds.

Vision is a perception... Since it is an internal and personal
mind-picture, every individual blends with an organizational vision his or her own expectations, aspirations, conditions, experiences, hopes and fears. An organization will
contain numerous interpretations of its vision. That is why
the clarity of "the original picture" is essential; otherwise
"the copies" people take from the original may become too
fuzzy. This is the reason for a visionary process within an
organization. It is through accurate communications that
personal visions are created, clarified and linked to the
institutional vision.

Is vision a viable concept?

Warren Bennis, one of the most distinguished and interna-
tionally known authorities on leadership, has found that,
"The single defining quality of leaders is their ability to create and realize a vision" (1993). Vision is a powerful and far-
reaching idea. Defining it is necessary, but not sufficient to
achieving success. As Bennis says, the vision also needs to
be "realized."

George Bush called visionary thinking, "that vision thing."
Maintaining this reactive mode in his presidential campaign
helped him to lose the election.

Louis Gerstner, new chairman of IBM, said in the press in
July 1993 that, "The last thing IBM needs now is a vision."
The very next day, July 28, 1993, the Wall Street Journal
printed that, "IBM has an accountant for a CEO" (Miller, M.
and Hays, L., 1993). Several chief executives who were
interviewed for the article, raised their eyebrows and
wondered. Even if Gerstner meant to say that some other
decisions have priority because of urgency, such as liquida-
tion of some fixed assets, a non-visionary comment is not
what is expected from a top executive. It was several
months before Business Week, in November 1993, could
report what Gerstner's vision for IBM actually looked like.

Jack Welch, CEO of General Electric, reinforces what Bennis
says by observing that, "Tomorrow's leader leads through
vision" (Bennis, 1993).

But even more important than the *ability* to turn vision into action is what Bennis describes as, "...the *responsibility* (of a leader) to transform that vision into reality," (italics ours). A leader is the driving force behind a firm's achievements. It is not enough for a leader to create a vision; a leader has the duty to *implement* that vision.

Michael Porter of Harvard University, author of the three most widely quoted books on strategic management, expresses this need very directly (1990):

> *"Real corporate leaders believe in change. They possess an insight into how to alter competition, and they do not accept constraints in carrying it out. Leaders energize their organizations to meet competitive challenges, to serve demanding needs, and above all, to keep progressing... Leaders also think in international terms, not only in measuring their true competitive advantage but in setting strategy to enhance and extend it."*

Vision may be the most powerful tool a leader has at his disposal. Great leaders have always been masters of vision. While George Bush's "vision thing" did not qualify him as a great leader or help him win the election, another president, John F. Kennedy, carved his name into the history books by setting a vision for the nation in 1961: "We will send a man to the moon by 1970." Some of the greatest leaders possess a vision which continues to inspire people beyond their life times. Martin Luther King still inspires us with his dream even today. Gandhi's legacy lives long after his death.

There are many visions in an organization

Corporate vision should be a source of inspiration, a basis for decision making and a coordinating point for action. Even the best vision loses its power, if it is not properly interpreted or understood within the organization:

Functional vision empowers corporate vision... What does the corporate vision mean for marketing, what does it mean for the human resource function or for accounting systems? A change in corporate vision leads to many changes in the organization. If the visions built by the various organizational functions are not aligned with the overall institutional vision, implementation is in jeopardy.

Division can create disintegration or integration... When companies decentralize, they hope that their organization will maintain the same structural and cultural integrity that it had before decentralization. That seldom happens. All too often, decentralization leads to disintegration. By managing the visionary process effectively, top management can integrate divisional thinking while decentralizing the organization.

Every team needs a vision... Organizations are full of teams. The customary corporate top team, divisional management teams, and functional teams have been joined by cross-functional teams, client teams, departmental teams, project teams and so on. It is essential that every team have a vision that:

- Is aligned with the larger corporate vision

- Is directed toward cooperation rather than competition

- Is reflected by the goals of individual team members

- Is commonly understood, interpreted and internalized

It all boils down to individual vision…When an individual can see personal benefit, either psychological or material, in the common vision, and it is consistent with his fundamental, core beliefs, then the probability of signing on and committing to implementation is high.

Whole brain visioning

Visions have no power if they are not vivid illustrations of our preferred future. As such, they must "speak" to the various functions of our minds that evaluate choices and enable us to make good decisions. In the Via Model, we speak of whole brain visioning as a process that creates such vivid pictures of the preferred future that consequent attitudes and behaviors are naturally aligned with vision achievement. This visioning is achieved by anchoring the "mind picture" in four aspects of brain functioning.

In this way, we create a vision that can be understood by all main functions of the brain. In the development of whole brain visioning, we have applied the findings of brain research as well as the work of Ned Herrmann (1990).

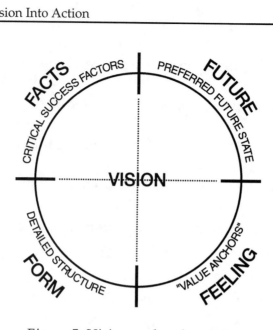

Figure 5: Vision anchor descriptors

A compelling vision is anchored in:

Facts... Fact anchoring secures a vision to reality. It does us no good to vision about a future in which we evolve into purple grasshoppers. By using actual data, and extrapolating out to the furthest realistic extremes, we can firmly anchor our vision to the achievable.

In our model, fact anchoring happens in the upper left part of the brain, which is described as quantitative, logical and analytical.

Future... Future anchoring has occurred when one can clearly see, like watching a picture, how the future will unfold if the vision is fulfilled.

Note: Anchoring a vision to the past only leads to reactionary thinking that lacks innovation and creativity.

In our whole brain model, future anchoring happens in the upper right part of the brain, which is described as intuitive and visual.

Feelings... Emotional anchoring of a vision has a particularly strong impact on human attitude and behavior. Deep emotional anchoring is possible when a vision is tied to our values. Value anchoring is the strongest of all moorings, enabling people to achieve the seemingly impossible.

> **Value anchored visions serve the essence of the person.**

In our model, emotional anchoring happens in the lower right part of the brain.

Form... Form anchoring secures a vision to the "doable," enabling the visionary to see the steps necessary to carry out the vision. Form anchoring occurs in the lower left portion of the brain.

If the future image is a vision that is firmly value-anchored, it can color everything an individual does. It becomes an inner coordinating program. However, visions that are unevenly anchored can be dangerous, because they hinder one from seeing the realities of the world, for example, occasionally, managers start to believe in partial solutions, like cost cutting or the newest management fad, in such an extreme way that they become incontestable truisms.

By developing an institutional vision, an organization sets its very core and foundation. By communicating it, an organization creates a coordinating force that can align people's thinking and actions in a common direction. By living its purpose daily, an organization energizes its people to efforts that exceed any conventional expectations.

Chapter Six

Visionary Leadership

*The soul never thinks
without a picture.*

Aristotle

Orchestrating a guiding purpose

It is no longer sufficient for leaders simply to have a strong sense of direction or even a clear vision. Whereas in the past, stakeholders searched for clarity and direction, it now appears they want to participate in the process of crafting a vision which will influence and shape a compelling future for the organization. The importance of visioning cannot be overstated. Yet, in the complexity of today's business environment, it is the *orchestration of the vision* or the *crafting of a guiding purpose* that emerges as the key visionary leadership challenge.

The following excerpt from General Electric's Management Values (1993) reinforces this need for orchestration of vision.

"GE Leaders—Always with Unyielding Integrity:

Create a Clear, Simple, Reality-Based, Customer-Focused Vision and are able to Communicate it to All Constituencies."

Consider for a moment the scope of the challenge of articulating a clear vision for a global organization with hundreds of business units, thousands of employees, a multitude of strategic objectives, and a host of national and organizational cultures and subcultures.

Yet, while orchestration of vision is foremost to leaders, it is not always first on the minds of other people in the organization. Most people in organizations these days are so overwhelmed with their daily routines and difficulties that an institutional vision is seen as "one of the last things we need around here." People are having sufficient difficulty with their own personal futures, let alone that of the institution for which they work. The development of an organizational vision is frequently seen as a waste of time or as unproductive or unnecessary work. The first hurdle a visionary leader must overcome is this skepticism. During difficult, recessionary times, vision might appear as so much "pie in the sky," yet in reality, it is crucial to organizational survival. The leader must be able to address questions such as, "Why do we need vision?" and "Why should I get involved?"

While most leaders agree with the necessity to create a guiding purpose for the organization, they are in a quandary as to how to accomplish the task. We are frequently asked, "What is the process for orchestrating the development and articulation of a vision?   Give us a visioning process that will work."

A visioning process

A good visioning process should be a synthesis of the best practices available for assisting senior management teams define and express a corporate vision for their organization's future.

Vision is value-anchored will.

It should focus on issues specific to each unique customer situation and draw from the real challenges and issues faced by the senior management team.

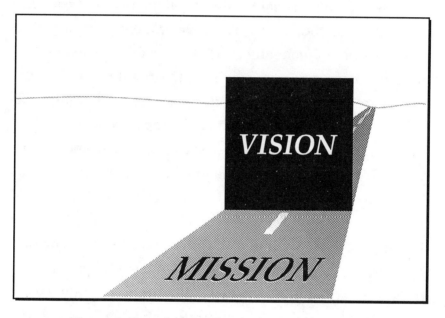

Figure 1: Translating Vision into business terms

Key Player analysis

The ultimate failure of any organization occurs when it fails to serve its key players. Many organizations state that the most important key player is the customer. The International Management and Leadership Survey confirms this (LSI, 1992). Major key players and their relative ranking may be seen on the next chart.

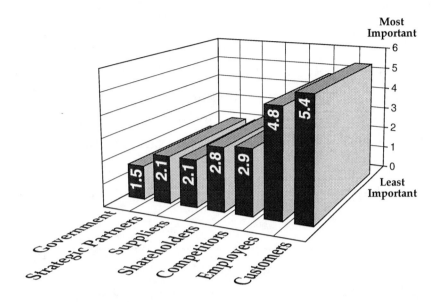

Figure 2: Key players by rank of importance

Real data and solid strategic thinking are critical success factors to a visioning process. Before beginning, one should conduct an analysis of the key players that surround the group. These key players would include customers, employees, suppliers, competitors, government offices, etc. This analysis is necessary to provide real data about the organization. Armed with this data, the management team can do the strategic thinking necessary to devise the transformation.

Developing visionary scenarios

Scenarios for an organization's future may be developed during the process. Each scenario should lead the group progressively closer to an operable vision.

Scenario 1

The "AS-IS" Picture is an image of the organization projected into the future without addressing any of today's problems. This is sometimes called the "Vision with No Action." This is a very important image to create in the minds of the management team because it essentially asks, "Do we really need to change anything?" Usually this generates a lot of energy to continue with the visioning process.

> **The pain of remaining the same**
> **must become greater than the pain of change.**

Scenario 2

The "SHOULD-BE" Picture is an image of the group with all of the current problems solved. This is sometimes called the "Action into Vision" scenario. In this case, the group creates an achievable image of the organization and sets some strategy to ease current organizational pain. This scenario generally looks pretty good to the team, and some of the more practical members will be ready to adopt it as the working vision for the organization. It is easy to be satisfied with this short-term picture, especially if it takes the heat off of the immediate leadership dilemmas. However, top executive leaders and their organizations cannot afford to be satisfied with short-term visions.

Scenario 3

The "COULD-BE" Picture is an expression of the management team's collective image (their will and values) for the organization. It is an expression of what they could really do with the organization if they could get everyone working together toward a preferred future. This is often called the "Vision into Action" scenario.

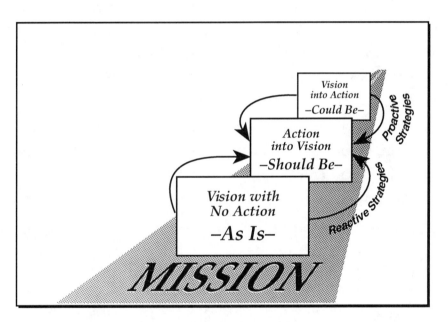

Figure 3: The three visions:
Vision with No Action,
Action into Vision,
and Vision into Action.

The working vision

As a result of constructing three time-bound vision scenarios, the management team can begin to see that a workable vision might be established by combining the best elements of Scenarios 2 and 3. Their "working" vision for the future of the organization will begin to take shape. It should be noted that it is important to test this working vision against key players' wants, needs and expectations.

Articulating the working vision to Key Players

It is important to construct a communication package which captures both the key players analysis that was done before the Vision Workshop and the Working Vision that was developed. This package is then used as a vehicle to engage key players in a dialogue about the preferred future of the organization—the New Business Idea. This dialogue is one of the critical success factors for the new vision. It will also greatly assist the speed of implementation. If this key player dialogue process is established before the vision is finalized, the vision has a much higher probability of being effectively implemented and for it to have influence on the decisions and actions of the key players.

Pearce and Robinson (1991) list the numerous key players that can make claims on an organization: creditors, employees, customers, suppliers, governments, unions, competitors, local committees and the general public.

Preparing for dialogue with Key Players—
Matching the "New Business Idea" with the Key Players

Dialogue with key customers, employees and other stakeholders is a critical step. Sometimes it is helpful to anticipate their resistance and acceptance of certain parts of the new business idea. The Via Model, which was explained in chapter 5, can serve as a useful model for this analysis.

The fourth level of the Via Model matches the organization's new business idea with its existing key players. By overlaying this match on a business transformation, we can see that any within- and between-organizational turbulence can begin to be bridged.

By taking the business idea and thinking about the various parts of the Via Model, it is possible to see the impact of that business idea on the vision, strategy, values and culture of the key players' organizations.

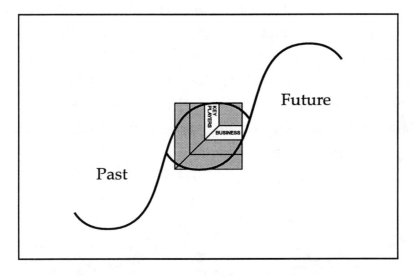

Figure 4: Beginning to bridge the gap

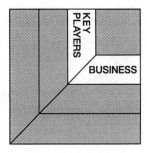

Figure 5: The fourth level of the Via Model

The evolving idea

Once the new business idea has been formulated, leaders often make the mistake of assuming that it will be implemented in the same form. However, this is rarely so. The
idea is remolded and shaped by the influences of the key
players of the business, much as a ball of clay might be
formed by the fingers of a potter. The new business idea is
still the new business idea, just as the clay is still clay.
However, it may take on slightly different form, depending
on the strength of each influence.

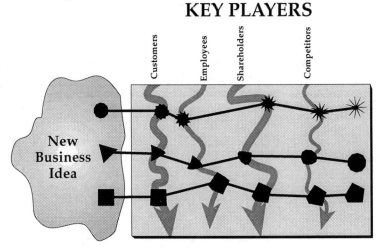

Figure 6: Shaping the new business idea

By ensuring that the new business idea matches with the key players' expectations and needs, the turbulence of business transformations can be bridged, intra- and inter-organizational teaming can be facilitated and the development of an organizational vision of lasting benefit may be accomplished.

Visionary leadership

On the visionary level, the same maxims hold true as on other levels of leadership.

A leader cannot give what he/she doesn't have.

A leader cannot give a vision to an organization, if he/she doesn't have one; the leader cannot renew the business idea, if there is no idea in mind. The visionary process starts from within, but, as we have described, it should involve others "early and often."

There is no commitment without participation.

Leading at the visionary level requires persistence, determination in the face of resistance, and a strong belief in the future. Visionary leaders must:

- Create a new and inspiring future for an organization, function or team and ensure the key players are committed

- Effectively communicate the vision throughout the organization

- Assist in implementation of the vision by interpreting it with different functions, groups and individuals

- Practice what is being preached—"live the talk."

It has been shown that employees see top management as the most powerful driving force behind vision. (Beer, Eisenstat, and Spector, 1990). Vision can energize the organization, but to what action? Strategic leadership, our topic for the next chapter, gives life to our picture of the preferred future.

Chapter Seven

Strategic Leadership:
The Change Engines

*The leader's role is to release energy
and to put the organization into
purposeful motion.*

Paul Galvin,
Late Founder and Chairman
Motorola, Inc.

Matching strategies to organizational culture

Strategy may be defined as the general scheme for the conduct of business.

Strategy = creating success potential
Implementing = turning potential into profit

Strategy is a more structured concept than the business idea, and it encompasses the "how," whereas, the business idea tells about "what." However, without the definitive influence of corporate culture, formulating strategy is only a management process.

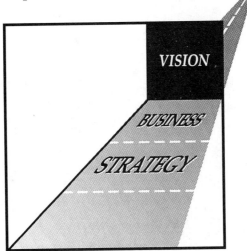

Figure 1: Strategy—the management process

Once we add culture, that often hidden and unmentioned aspect of organizational life, we have a leadership process.

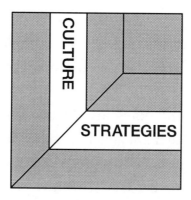

Figure 2: Matching strategy and culture—
a crucial part of the leadership process

Personality reflects an individual's character. Culture reflects an organization's "personality." Corporate or organizational culture is based on habits developed over time and consists of the beliefs, values and habits of the people within the organization. These beliefs and habits may vary from unit to unit within an organization, depending on many factors.

Culture represents our psychological past.

Edgar Schein (1985), a widely published author in the behavioral sciences, believes that the term "culture" should be reserved for the deeper unconscious level of *basic assumptions* and *beliefs* which are shared by members of an organization and that define in a basic "taken for granted" fashion, an organization's view of itself and its environment. We have found culture to encompass a company's habits, practices and ways of doing things as well as Schein's deeper basic assumptions and beliefs.

Jay Lorsch of Harvard University (1986) defines organizational culture as the shared beliefs top managers in a company have about how they should manage themselves and other employees, and how they should conduct their business(es). Although beliefs are often invisible they have a major impact on the managers thoughts and actions. We believe that while Lorsch is correct in his emphasis on top management beliefs, these beliefs only constitute a small, albeit powerful, portion of the overall culture of an institution.

> **The core of an organization's culture
> is the culture of its management/leadership.**

Leaders reflect the culture of their organizations. If a leader has held her position for some time, her strengths and weaknesses are remarkably mirrored in the organizational culture. Since leaders and managers generally have more power in an organization than other individuals, they tend to influence it more.

Vision, strategies and goals represent our future, whereas culture represents our collective past. The place where our future and past intersect and collide is where leadership is needed.

> **Organizational culture may be thought of as "how we
> do business around here."**

The organizational culture iceberg

Consider the metaphor of organization as iceberg. The visible part represents only 10 percent of the whole. The dominant part, the other 90 percent is hidden, submerged from view.

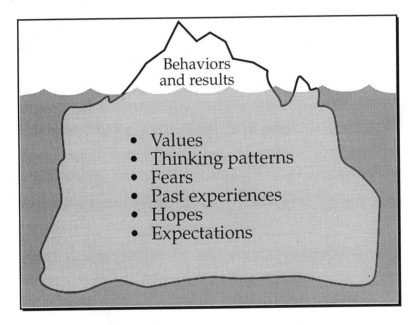

Figure 3: The organization as iceberg

The visible 10 percent represents actual behaviors and results. These are strongly affected by the elements listed in the hidden 90 percent.

Organizational programming, or, as we have defined it, organizational culture, steers observable behaviors; two parts of an iceberg cannot move in different directions, they are one and the same piece of ice. Just by looking at the iceberg in the figure, we can see why managers who do not want or know how to deal with the deeper levels of organization *fail* in managing change. Business-as-usual focuses merely on the observable part, the measurable results. By addressing the deeper issues with an open leadership process, a leader may remarkably increase the amount of effective change.

> **A leader improves her chances of changing the 90 percent by effectively influencing the 10 percent.**

When there is a match between an organization's culture and the strategies selected to carry out its new business idea, then implementation is greatly facilitated and easily reinforced. However, when strategies conflict with an organizations beliefs and values then the likelihood of success is almost nil.

> **The moment of truth for a strategy is when it confronts an organization's culture.**

Company culture should never be underestimated. It can either ensure successful implementation, or kill the entire business idea.

The new strategic leader

We have looked at the process for diagnosing the match between the strategic initiatives that have been crafted to implement the chosen direction changes for the organization and the existing organizational culture. In the diagram below it can be seen that culture is like a magnetic field that either attracts or repels the new strategic initiatives. It is an invisible field that exerts influence and causes strategic initiatives to begin to take form—to evolve as we stated in the previous chapter. This cultural field sets up a "gauntlet" for the new initiative. And, as any experienced executive can tell you, the culture wins most of the battles when strategy and culture collide.

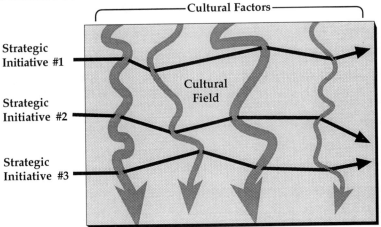

Figure 4: The life of strategic initiatives
as they run the gauntlet of the Cultural Field

The New Strategic Leader will be a navigator, crafting new strategic initiatives and making them "navigable"—this means that they will be sufficiently robust to survive the run through the cultural "gauntlet".

In addition, the New Strategic Leader will be constantly "walking the talk," working to make the organization more "change ready." This means that there will be a conscious effort to also craft initiatives that will work on the organizational culture to make future strategic initiatives increasingly easier to implement.

> **With each major change a conscious effort must be made to build a heritage of successful change. This can be capitalized on when the organization needs to alter course in the future.**

The interesting thing about this cultural field is that it is like a flowing river. It is constantly changing shape to meet the demands and challenges posed as new initiatives confront it. With the implementation of each new initiative it is never the same again, it is a constantly flowing and changing force, and it is a powerful tool of the new Strategic Leader.

If this cultural field is rooted in the history, values, fears and expectations of the organization it is truly one of the organization's most potent resources. During the past several years there has been a lot written about organizational learning. It has been pioneered by people like Chris Argyris in his book—*Learning, Reasoning and Action* (1982) and Peter Senge in his book, *The Fifth Discipline* (1990). They have discussed ideas and concepts regarding the importance of the people within an organization being able to learn. In fact, the organizations that have individuals who can learn and adapt to rapid changes have the only truly sustainable competitive advantage. While these books and their authors discuss "what" is needed, there is little "how-to" advice given to the practicing manager who wants to be able to promote organizational learning. Most of the practical tools of organizational change and learning have come from the leading edge organizations that have tried and improved methods for producing organizational learning and change.

Lower level change efforts may also be viewed as having to run the gauntlet of the cultural field. Team goals and individual tasks, given that they must be accomplished by members of the organization, are also strongly influenced by corporate values, beliefs and ways of doing things. Goals and tasks may be more specific than organizational strategies, but within their particular contexts they contribute to the formation of team and individual "cultures" within an organization.

A new paradigm is needed for negotiating the operating environment of business today, one which enables the organization to respond instantaneously and in perfect rhythm with changes in that environment. New ways of thinking and acting are evident in the most prolific and rapidly-growing market segments. This includes such industries as semiconductors, information technology, communications and entertainment.

For these industries, and increasingly for the rest of the world, it takes too long to study, select a course of action and then implement a plan. By the time these tasks are completed, the game will have changed leaving the less nimble companies behind. Mike Birck, founder and CEO of Tellabs, has expressed his frustration with the traditional approach to setting strategic direction in the highly turbulent telecommunications industry saying that, "by the time that you get all the traditional analysis completed, the marketplace will have left you behind."

This has led to the search for a strategic process that is less cumbersome and that allows for continuous learning. With the help of Mike Birck and others, we have developed the Change Engine as the basic tool kit for the strategic navigator that wants to turn his organization into a learning machine.

> **A Strategic Navigator must enable the organization to change course effortlessly and continuously, matching wave for wave.**

What is the prescription for success? How does one become a strategic navigator and create an organization that can learn instantaneously and move in perfect harmony with changes in the environment?

The basic requirement of strategic navigation is a maneuverable craft, one readily piloted regardless of the conditions. A basic rule for heavy weather sailing is not to lose headway. You must keep the organization moving in order to be able to steer. A good strategic navigator provides three essential ingredients for the organization.

• **Steerage**—In a fluid environment, one has to be able to steer the craft. Large organizations can no longer "stay the course", but must learn to be immediately responsive to the helm. As a strategic navigator, the leader must be able to operate the steering gear—the levers of change—that will enable the organization to change course effortlessly.

• **A Generator**—the generator provides the electricity for the ship. The leader must release the energy which is bound up in the organizational culture, structure and politics. Many leaders try to control energy rather than release it. This is the death of strategic change.

> **It is necessary to effectively control today's business but it takes the release of energy to create tomorrow's.**

The uncertainty of today's realities has produced much fear and insecurity. All the media attention surrounding "right sizing," all the mergers and acquisitions of the 80's and a poor economy in the 90's have combined to unhook the individual from the organization. Organizational cultures are disintegrating and internal violence is the result. The strategic navigator must have a process to rehook the individual to the organization.

All organizations are crying for speed. *Tempo* is speed over time; speed achieved through the people who make up an organization. Increasing tempo will only come from reaching the individual.

Tempo is the speed of an organization achieved through its people.

• **Propulsion**—Leaders provide the main propulsion, the overall institutional purpose and mission to which individual effort is tied. It is the leaders that create the much needed velocity that put the organization into purposeful motion. As we defined earlier, purposeful motion consists of those decisions and actions that drive an organization towards an anticipated and planned-for future. Leaders enable the organization to make headway by setting an example—providing a role model. They also can knock down barriers to change in real time. This can be accomplished by a process like the General Electric "Work-Out"—a process to create velocity in the organization. Velocity is speed over distance, or the speed achieved by a business over the long haul through the changes made by its leaders. By incisively making or enabling key decisions, taking quick and responsive action, and knocking down systemic defects, leaders enable the organization to maneuver swiftly toward the future.

Leaders provide sustained velocity through visionary change.

Illustrating the navigational challenge

We have described how people bring the influences of their past to new situations. A gap opens where experiences, education, upbringing and culture collide with the future plans of an organization. This gap may be illustrated as a separation between the two sides of the Via model.

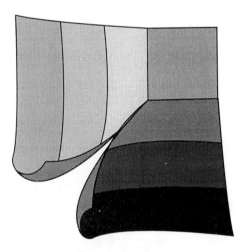

Figure 5: The leadership challenge

Traditionally, leaders have attempted to stitch this gap together with their individual leadership capabilities, using the one-to-one approach to integrate the business and people issues. The *velocity* that they have been able to create has been, at times, insufficient in the face of increasing turbulence in the business environment. Transformations became painful, difficult and much too time-consuming.

A secondary approach to closing the gap was developed, utilizing training as the intervention. Unfortunately, long-

term results were not good, the effects of the training programs being short-lived. Tempo was not maintained.

**The traditional approach to transformation
is simply too slow.**

Relying on an organization's business-as-usual approach to
transformation was like using a needle and thread to stitch
the organization together.

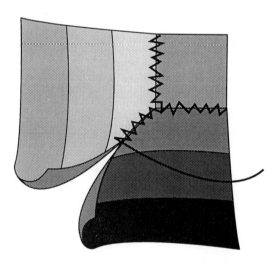

Figure 6: Stitching together the preferred future and the past.

The systems
approach to navigation

Viewing an organization as a set of interlinked systems may
provide a fresh perspective on the leader's role as navigator.
In order to close the described gap between the preferred fu-

ture and the culture and habits of the past, a leader might take a more systematic approach than the traditional "stitching" method.

> **The Via Change Engine runs continuously to close the gap between the future and the past.**

The Via Change Engine follows directly from the Via model's diagnostic strategy/culture match. It provides a flexible and dynamic means of *constantly creating* the match and fit between future and past.

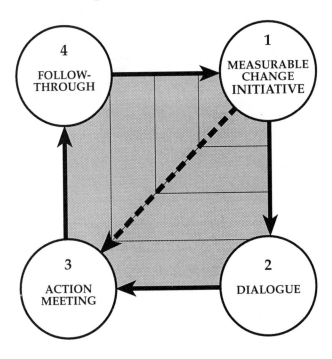

Figure 7: The Via Change Engine is a systematic approach to strategic navigation.

The systematic approach is akin to utilizing a zipper or velcro, rather than needle and thread, to link the people and business sides of an organization. It is quicker, easier to use, adjustable, and may be readily opened or closed so that individual parts may be altered or repaired as necessary.

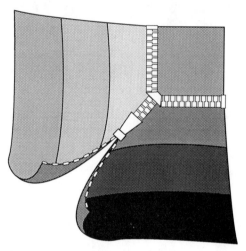

Figure 8: The systematic approach to strategic navigation—using a zipper on the Via model.

Describing the
Via Change Engine

The Via Change Engine is a four-stage iterative and cyclical leadership process designed to ensure that organizational renewal is continuous and Strategic Initiatives are implemented. This will enable the organization to behave like the Terminator II, mentioned in Chapter 3, adapting instantaneously and continuously to a rapidly changing environment.

Just imagine for a moment what your organization would have if it could adapt instantly to change. Imagine how responsive you would be to customer needs and what kind of employer you could become if the organization could be that flexible. If the environment of the next decade will be as turbulent as we expect it to be, ability to move with the flow could mean the difference between those organizations that survive and those that do not.

The initiatives of change

The drivers of organizational change are strategic initiatives. Once a direction has been selected, the organization's leaders have to decide how they want to move in the direction they have chosen.

Transformational change affects everyone and involves the entire system and its structures. Therefore, it is essential that the new strategic direction for the organization be articulated into strategic initiatives that are navigable.

So what are the characteristics that make navigable strategic initiatives? Navigable means that as a leader you can steer them as they run the gauntlet of the organizational culture. It is a given that the organizational culture will resist new initiatives. These initiatives are the new packages of the change process. In order for the organization to change, these initiatives must be successfully implemented. It does not make any sense to even attempt implementing any strategic initiative that is not sufficiently robust to withstand the organizational culture. So how do you make your initiatives change ready? How do you make them navigable?

Via Change Engine

Stage 1: A measurable change initiative

Each strategic initiative should be framed by the Via model so that purpose is defined, vision described, enablers (strategies) are selected, the cultural diagnosis completed, and implementation by teams and individuals planned. However, before framing the initiative, it is useful to look at the characteristics that will make it navigable:

The vital few

It is essential that the change process be articulated into the vital few initiatives and measures. If leaders give the organization too many new things to learn all at once, chaos will result.

This can be illustrated in a case example. We recently worked on a project in an automobile company employing 225,000 employees worldwide. The organization was having some problems and was about to report an operating loss for the first time in its history. In order to resolve the problems that had developed, they designed 20 Strategic Initiatives to restore the company to competitiveness. In order to implement these initiatives cross-functional teams were formed and 20 of the top leaders in the company were appointed to lead the teams. You can imagine the result....Chaos. The senior managers were perplexed. The fact is that the organization could not do 20 new things at once. "You mean that our organization of 225,000 people cannot accomplish 20 new things?" The fact is that those 20 initiatives represented millions of new tasks once they had trickled down the organization. In addition, the associates had to continue doing all the traditional tasks of running the business. It is important to remember that changing an organization is like trying to change the tire on a moving automobile!

Impossible goals

Leaders need to help their organizations do what seems to be impossible. By setting impossible goals the leaders can set the standards to which they want the organization to aspire. It is the leaders' duty to take the organization to a place where it would not ordinarily go on its own.

A good example of this is the Six Sigma quality initiative which was successfully implemented by Motorola during the 1980s. Motorola's survival was threatened when faced with the competitive threats of the Japanese in many of its traditional markets. Bob Galvin, then CEO, realized that the only way to respond to the threat was to beat them at their own game. He had to take all the good features of the proud Motorola culture and focus on improving quality and customer satisfaction. The quality initiative at Motorola struggled during the early stages of its implementation. Then in about the mid-1980s the initiative was renamed Six Sigma. This meant that Motorola products would be virtually perfect. It was believed that if Six Sigma could be achieved, lower costs and increased customer satisfaction would result. Many people believed that Six Sigma was an impossible goal. None the less, the executives held their ground and made the achievement of steadily increasing quality and customer satisfaction part of the regular review process. These vital metrics would be reviewed every quarter before sales and profits. In addition the results would be tied to executive compensation. And the rest is history. The successful implementation of Six Sigma did in fact reduce costs and improve customer satisfaction. In addition, the company established a global reputation for quality and is teaching the Six Sigma process through Motorola University to other organizations around the world. Six Sigma is an excellent example of a Reach Out Initiative.

Another unique feature of Six Sigma is that the goal is built into the name of the initiative. In other words Six Sigma is simultaneously the name and the goal. This keeps it visible and can serve as a rallying point for the organization.

Sustained executive sponsorship

It is virtually impossible to implement change without significant and continuous top management support. Strategic initiatives must have the kind of support implied in this title to be successful. Organizational change is difficult even under the most favorable circumstances. If there is not strong executive sponsorship, forget it. Sponsorship must be visible and the initiative must be an organizational mandate. Without these ingredients, organizational entropy will win, the pressing priorities of running the business will take over and no change will happen. Bottom line, if you want your change initiatives to be implemented they must be "high visibility imperatives." The Six Sigma example above is a good illustration. Quarterly reviews before sales and profits and the link to executive compensation kept it in front of everyone. Another good example is the "Quality is Job one" initiative at Ford which, as a rallying point for employees, caused significant improvement. If you do not have a burning platform, create one. As Bob Galvin of Motorola says, "if we had not had the Japanese threat, we should have created it. It reinvented our business."

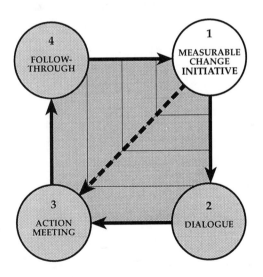

Figure 9: Creating the change initiative, stage one

Did you ever try playing tennis without lines or a net? Try it some time. The game is reduced to merely hitting a ball back and forth. You will quickly get bored and stop playing, or you will invent a new game! This is exactly what is needed when trying to implement organizational change. When a metric is established, you transform your strategic initiative into a measurable process.

No metrics ...No movement

Generally, when introducing a significant organizational change, we are trying to change the game. The only problem is that we often forget to redefine the rules. Think about it. Most strategic initiatives are rolled out with a lot of fanfare, but there are no parameters built into the initiative and no score card or score keeping mechanism. Soon the organization loses interest in playing the new game and it is back to more of the same. It is essential to put a lot of thought into the measurement plan of new strategic initiatives.

Create a purposeful disturbance

Many organizational change efforts become an exercise in activity and not much accomplishment. There is a flurry of activity. There is the feeling of new momentum. Lots of workshops are given, speeches are made, and money is spent only to fail in getting the desired results. It is therefore the duty of top management to define the standards expected by the change. If we follow along with our example of Six Sigma, the standard was very clear. The top management of Motorola wanted 99.999997% perfection. That means 3 defects per million. Once the standard was set and the review mechanisms were in place, they could leave the "how" of achieving the standard to the individual operating unit. In addition, with a standard, you can measure back from the vision. With metrics that measure improvement only, you see a lot of pretty charts demonstrating improvement, but no real results. If you want results, and not just wasted motion, do not play the improvement game—set the standard, create a purposeful disturbance and get a report of the errors. Only then can you measure true results.

> **Learning occurs whenever errors are detected and corrected.**
> **Chris Argyris**

Via Change Engine
Stage 2: Dialogue

Due to continuously changing business circumstances and changes in key player wants and needs, culture change is a dynamic, ever moving state rather than a position that, once achieved, is maintained in equilibrium. This is reflected in the looping design of the Via Change Engine.

The role of Dialogue in the process is seen in the graphic below. Once everyone involved in the change process has had a proper orientation to the new initiative and the issues have been surfaced, it is time to develop a deep understanding of the "why" behind the issues. New initiatives that call for significant change are filled with ambiguity and uncertainty. It is important to engage the participants in a dialogue that addresses their perceptions and brings clarity to the plan.

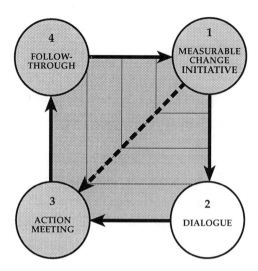

Figure 10: Dialogue, Stage Two

Dialogue creates openness and trust.

Through genuine dialogue, organizations can create a climate of openness and mutual trust. This process is necessary to drive the fear and uncertainty out of the organization, that can, and often do, paralyze purposeful action and hinder the change process.

Internal Agendas and your Business

People don't always do what they say they will. We have all experienced this in our lives. Inconsistencies between words and actions create frustration, promote a lack of trust, surface negative attitudes and contribute to the ineffectiveness within organizations.

Harvard's Chris Argyris, who has studied the results of these inconsistencies for 30 years says, "Although people do not always behave congruently with what they say, they do behave congruently with their theories-in-use (internal agenda, internal truth, internal dialogue) (1992). One can easily find many examples where clear business intentions are paralyzed by unspoken internal dialogues. Passive/aggressive behaviors and sabotage occur when mismatches between internal agendas and business objectives are not resolved.

A recent survey conducted with senior executives in 13 countries revealed that nearly one third of the leaders were not really committed to the strategies they were responsible for implementing (LSI, 1992). If this is the "internal dialogue" of the people at the top, imagine what it is like further down in the organization.

The idea of "internal agendas" is a powerful concept. As leaders, we need to understand the "internal truths," "mental models" or "internal images of how the world works" in order to be effective in our businesses. The dialogue process works by surfacing the "internal talk" so that it can be dealt with effectively.

Why discussion is not enough

Discussion comes from the same root word as percussion, which is "quatere"—to shake, and we all know that percussion instruments create noise. Human interaction in organizations often seems like percussion—a lot of noise created. This is particularly true in times of change.

Dialogue on the other hand comes from two Greek words, Dia (which means two) and Logos (which means interaction, with meaning flowing through). Peter Senge defines dialogue as "a free flow of meaning between people" (1990). He adds, "the purpose of dialogue is to reveal the incoherence in each other's thoughts", and "in dialogue people become the observers of their own and others thoughts."

The purpose of dialogue is to reveal the incoherence in each other's thoughts.
Peter Senge

Discussion, although a necessary counterpart to dialogue, is not sufficient. Dialogue is a means to discovering new points of view. Peter Senge's definition of dialogue gives a new, deeper and more challenging meaning to the concept of dialogue. As Senge points out, "Dialogue leads to a mature communication process that is needed in complex and changing situations."

Some benefits of dialogue include:

- development of deep trust
- richer understanding
- less rigidity in defending one's position
- creation of unique relationships

Dialogue does not always mean changing your own opinion. A person with strong dialogue skills can be seen as a "master of suspending one's own position" rather than being "held by one's own position."

At this point, people usually say, "OK, I believe this dialogue stuff sounds important, but how do you conduct an effective dialogue session with others?"

How to conduct an effective dialogue

Step 1: Create Understanding

The first hurdle to an effective dialogue about a new strategic initiative is understanding that initiative. It sounds simple enough, but many of the implementation problems surrounding new initiatives are due to a lack of understanding of the intent of the initiative—why the company has decided to do it and what is in it for everyone involved. Until people have this kind of basic orientation, it is very difficult for them to engage in an effective dialogue, much less play an active role in effective implementation.

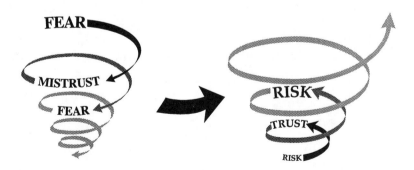

Figure 11: The cycles of trust and mistrust

Step 2: Build Trust

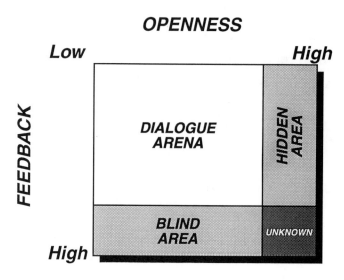

Figure 12: Openness and feedback skills
can expand the available dialogue arena.

Perhaps the biggest hurdle to effective dialogue and organizational change is *fear*. People are naturally suspicious of change efforts, especially with all of the initiatives that have led to the elimination of jobs and the loss of friends and coworkers. This leads to a lack of trust. When there is a lack of trust and/or large amounts of fear in the organization, change will be slow and painful. The skills needed to build trust in a dialogue session include 1) ability to create a climate that makes dialogue possible, 2) ability to deal with people's differing perceptions during the dialogue process, and 3) ability to get the dialogue process off on the right foot.

> **If you have failed to gain the commitment of others, you should assess your own approach to participation.**

Before trying to launch into a deep dialogue with others, you must determine if there is sufficient trust in the system to be able to talk openly about issues. Without trust, we will merely be engaging in a discussion or a monologue. It may take several attempts to overcome the "trust" hurdle with others. But, with the skills of openness and feedback, it is possible to create an arena where effective dialogue is possible with nearly everyone.

> **An error is any mismatch between intentions and actual consequences.**
> **Chris Argyris**

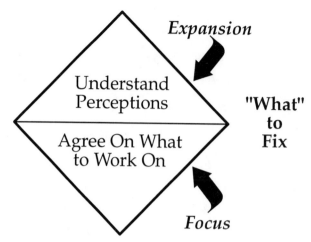

*Figure 13: The expansion and focus model of dialogue:
"What" to fix.*

Step 3: Dialogue "what" to fix

Achieving competence in dialogue facilitation is a key skill
for the leader of the future. It is easy to get lots of practice
since we get so many opportunities. Unfortunately, old
habits and pressing commitments keep our interactions with
others brief, and effective dialogue suffers.

To facilitate change, every manager should be prepared to
engage in constructive dialogue with the others involved in
the change process. Each one should be attempting to truly
understand the issues and perceptions that are behind the
responses to the new initiative. By the end of a dialogue
session, a manager should understand these differing perceptions and have some sense of the important issues to address in order to continue to build trust and to drive the implementation of the new initiative.

It is important to note that gaining competence at dialogue is a process not an event. Even if initial dialogue sessions are wildly successful, and everyone walks away feeling that progress is being made, it will take several iterations of the looping process for it to begin to create the dramatic improvements that are possible when effective dialogue is a dominant feature of the cultural field of an organization.

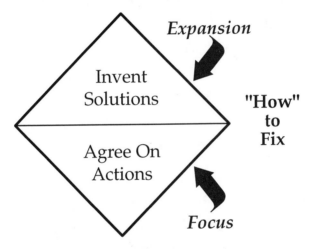

Figure 14: The expansion and focus model:
"How" to fix

Step 4: Dialogue "how" to fix

How many new strategic initiatives have you seen launched over the past five years? How many are still in force? Many were probably launched, but few were sustained. "Program Du Jour" is what some call it. Others call it strategic initiative gridlock.

Why are so many initiatives launched and so few actually realized? If dialogue sessions are effective, many new shared understandings will emerge and many issues will surface.

But natural skepticism about these processes will also arise. Unless all questions are answered and problems resolved, these issues, and others, will disappear into the organizational "black hole"—never to be discussed or resolved until next year's initiative puts them back on the table. This is a situation you want to avoid.

Arnold Schwarzenegger has been quoted as saying, "No one ever got big muscles from watching me lift weights. You have to do it yourself!" The same may be said about the issues that surface in the dialogue sessions. Action is essential. You must prioritize them, focus on the "vital few" to fix, and go fix them. This is the only way people will believe in the initiative and in the organization's ability to create real change.

> **It is essential to prioritize the problems or issues raised in dialogue, focus on the "vital few," and go fix them.**

Via Change Engine Stage 3: Action meeting— Real-time problem solving

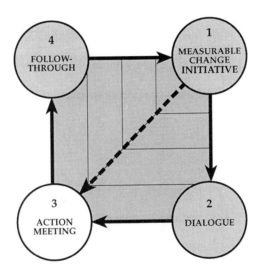

Figure 15: Action Meeting—Stage Three

It is now possible to see why large scale organizational change is so difficult. We began this process looking at the match between the strategic initiatives the organization is trying to implement and the culture of the institution. This led to the development of a *"vital few" initiatives* to drive strategic and cultural change. Key metrics were then developed around the initiatives to make them navigable. Once the initiative is "launched" the implementation process has begun.

We then covered the need to create a *dialogue* in and around the organization to give people the opportunity to begin to understand their perceptions and role changes in the new situation. As we discussed in the last section, this dialogue process gives the organization the opportunity to confront the "internal agendas" that are the silent killers of change. Once the dialogue process has begun in the organization, numerous issues will surface that need to be resolved. Some of the issues will be local and some of them will be organizational.

Local and Organizational Issues

Local issues may be defined as those that can be resolved within the sphere of influence of the team or individual involved in the dialogue. This does not mean that they control all the resources necessary to resolve the issue, but that they know how and where to go to influence those who do. The next figure shows, in an organizational context, what we mean by the local sphere of influence.

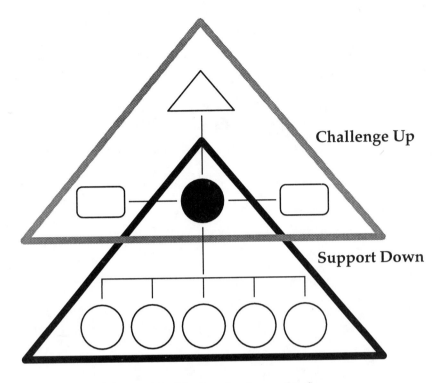

Figure 16: The local sphere of influence

Organizational Issues would be those that need to be escalated to be resolved. These are often "systemic" issues that
seem impossible to overcome. People usually feel helpless
when faced by a systemic issue and say things like "that's
our system," or "our system won't allow that to be done."
In order for the organization to prevent the frustration of a
huge pile of unresolved issues that will frustrate the change
process, there needs to be a way to confront and deal with
the larger organizational and systemic issues that can shut
down even the best of change efforts.

Work-Out—a continuous process of systemic change and leadership development to attain business objectives.

In order to create the needed changes in leadership and culture, General Electric, under the leadership of Jack Welch, pioneered the "Work-Out Process." Work-Out was designed as an evolutionary process that would begin with "small wins" that would eliminate unnecessary work and build confidence in the process. Work-Out would increase in intensity and scope until the eventual goal of making GE the "most productive company on earth" was accomplished. In the beginning, Work-Out was designed to:

- give a voice to all employees

- move decision making to the lowest level where a competent decision could be made

- permeate organization boundaries

- provide and reinforce team-based training, tools and information

- increase speed

- reduce bureaucracy

These are issues that many organizations are working to improve. However, for most managers, they are also very difficult to implement. Everyone can describe the problems, but when it comes to crafting a practical process to resolve these issues, people come up empty. Following the logic that it is important to "get the organization into purposeful motion," it is *not* essential that a perfect process be designed prior to implementation, but that one be *started and improved along the way.* This is exactly what has happened with Work-Out. Both Chris Cappy of Hollander, Kerrick and Cappy, and Dick Jelinek of General Electric have conducted many Work-Out sessions. They indicate that Work-Out has evolved to meet the changing needs of the various GE business units. The sharing of best Work-Out practices around the organization has caused it to improve into the powerful change technology that it is today.

Now that the background of the Work-Out has been described, we can focus on how one is conducted.

A typical GE Work-Out Town Meeting

The basic implementation of Work-Out has occurred in the Town Meeting, a powerful innovation for escalating, resolving and committing to action those issues that will improve the business. It is important to note that these sessions were designed to be hosted by business leaders, and to involve all participants in solving issues raised. The business leaders are put on the spot to commit to action on the recommendations—in real time. The slow and painful escalation process in traditional bureaucratic hierarchies has been the driver of development of the Town Meeting.

The role of leader has been in silent transition for the past decade, from one who tells to one who asks and enables.

Work-Out is the perfect medium for business leaders to exercise these new leadership behaviors and to be perceived as "asking and enabling" rather than telling.

What is the focus of a Town Meeting? What are some of the features that make the process so unique and powerful?

The typical town meeting has a Pre-Meeting phase during which key issues to be addressed are identified, expectations are communicated, the right people are selected, and the business leaders are prepared for their role in the session.

The Town Meeting is a *real time* problem-solving session that involves not only business leaders and employees, but also customers and suppliers, if necessary, to empower the process and get the right commitments. The basic purpose of any Work-Out is *action*. In turbulent times, speed is crucial. Because of this emphasis on action and speed, the name of the Work-Out session evolved into *Action Town Meeting* at GE. As such, it is a powerful change technology that can be applied to numerous businesses and situations.

The Action Town Meeting

The meeting itself would pursue an agenda similar to the following:

- Business Leadership kicks off the session and sets the challenge, making sure that expectations are aligned regarding the process and the intended outcomes.

- Teams are formed (7-10 per key issue) and some team-building experiences and problem-solving training are conducted to make the actual problem solving session more effective. This establishes the common tools and methods for working on the issues.

- The teams then move into facilitated problem-solving sessions, where they create solutions to the actual business and systemic issues surfaced in the dialogue sessions and prioritized for focus in this meeting. This phase ends with the development of recommendations.

- The session ends with the teams presenting their recommendations regarding the issues to the business leadership. The business leaders are then expected to commit to moving the process forward.

Following the meeting, it is essential that the process continue with Follow-up and Follow-through mechanisms established to ensure that commitments are kept. If the essential follow-through does not happen, the process will break down.

A successful Action Town Meeting results in:

- the opportunity for people to challenge business leadership to eliminate unproductive work, starting with reports, controls, approvals, meetings and practices that hinder the effective implementation of strategic initiatives

- business leaders listening and responding directly to their people at all levels

- elimination of unneeded work and controls

- managers empowering their people—with the focus on "what" not "how"

- real bureaucrats feeling threatened

- getting the business focused on what it really will take to win

Via Change Engine
Stage 4:
Follow-Through

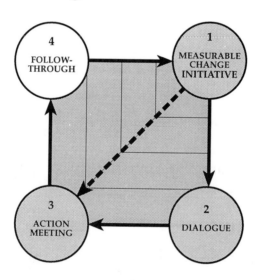

Figure 17: Follow-Through is the logical point
in the loop where all of the issues that have been surfaced
in the Dialogue and Action Meeting processes
should be resolved.

Follow-Through is one of the most powerful approaches to change that an organization can take. Although conceptually simple, in many cases, it has a stronger influence than even goal setting in the achievement of change and action.

Marshall Goldsmith, of Keilty Goldsmith and Company, recently conducted an excellent study of Fortune 500 companies. The study focused on the impact of follow-through on perceived leader effectiveness, following a 360 degree feedback process. It tells the story convincingly:

- The leaders who did not dialogue and did not follow through improved only sporadically:

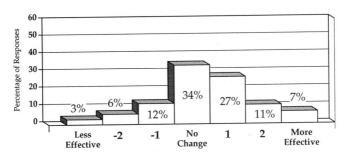

Leadership Effectiveness Scale: Group A

Figure 18: Leadership effectiveness without Follow-Through

- *All leaders* who engaged participants in a dialogue about their change goals, and followed through with them, were rated as better leaders within one year.

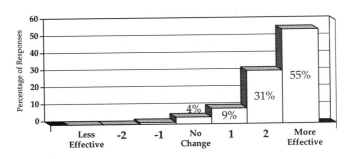

Leadership Effectiveness Scale: Group B

Figure 19: Leadership effectiveness with Follow-Through

- The difference in results between these two groups was clear and meaningful—even when both groups received the same training.

**Follow-through may be a leader's
most influential approach to creating results.**

This study has been replicated, using measured feedback to major account teams regarding their effectiveness with customers. Not surprisingly, the results are the same:

Account teams who: receive feedback; develop a simple action plan for improvement; discuss the plan with customers; conduct frequent, short, simple follow-through customer dialogues reporting progress in fixing the issues and achieving goals; and measure progress, almost invariably show *dramatic increases in perceived effectiveness*.

Account teams who do not engage in dialogue and follow-through show improvement that is only slightly greater than chance.

Make Follow-Through
part of the normal business rhythm

It has always been a mystery to us that strategic and operational metrics are part of different management feedback processes. For example, we want to improve quality or speed, yet the metrics are part of a process separate from sales and profits. The message is clear that people pay attention to what is measured and followed through on.

Therefore, it is important to include metrics for strategic change as a part of the normal operating reviews of the organization. For example, Motorola has established a practice which measures the standards and progress of change efforts against the standards for quality, customer satisfaction and cycle time improvements in every operating review. In fact, these metrics are discussed before sales and profits are factored in, in order to demonstrate executive commitment to strategic change.

New Roles for strategic leaders in dynamic organizations

If the Change Engine is used as the method for managing strategic change in an organization, then the new strategic leaders must begin to understand their roles in leading the process.

In order to articulate the new roles for the strategic leader, we have reviewed the literature and found two different views that seem to best summarize what is required.

The first viewpoint comes from a global study conducted by the International Consortium for Executive Development Research (1994). The study was conducted with 1200 global executives from such organizations as AT&T, British

Airways, Fiat Group, Siemens, Daimler-Benz, Ssang Yong and several others. The findings from this study can be summarized as follows:

The top five key organizational capabilities

- Be Organized around Customer Requirements

- Be Flexible to Meet New Competitive Conditions

- Be the Quality Leader

- Be the Customer Service Leader

- Have an Organizational Vision for the Future

The top five key leadership competencies

- Articulates a Tangible Vision, Values and Strategy

- Is a Catalyst for Strategic Change

- Gets Results—Manages Strategy into Action

- Empowers Others to Do Their Best

- Is Catalyst for Cultural Change

It was clear from the research that the Strategic Leader's role is in transition. The chart below articulates the changing nature of the role of strategic leaders in dynamic organizations:

From	To
• Setting a clear direction	• Orchestrating a guiding purpose
• Selecting a strategy	• Cultivating strategic agility
• Achieving competitive advantage	• Creating customer value
• Staying on course	• Enabling regeneration

Table 1: Competitive capabilities:
A changing framework for strategic leadership

The second viewpoint comes from an article in Chief Executive Magazine (1993), in which Jack Welch, CEO of General Electric, articulates the management values he expects from the leaders of the General Electric transformation.

GE Management values

GE Leaders—Always with Unyielding Integrity:

- Create a Clear, Simple, Reality-Based, Customer-Focused Vision and are Able to Communicate it Straight forwardly to all Constituencies.

- Reach/Set Aggressive Targets…Understand Accountability and Commitment and are Decisive.

- Have a Passion for Excellence…Hate Bureaucracy and all the Nonsense that comes with it.

- Have the Self-Confidence to Empower Others and Behave in a Boundaryless fashion...Believe in and are committed to Work-Out as a means of Empowerment...Are open to Ideas from Anywhere.

- Have, or Have the Capacity to Develop, Global Brains and Global Sensitivity, and are comfortable building Diverse Global Teams.

- Stimulate and Relish Change...Are not frightened or paralyzed by it...See Change as an Opportunity, Not a Threat.

- Have Enormous Energy and the Ability to Energize and Invigorate Others...Understand Speed as a Competitive Advantage and See the Total Organizational Benefits that can be derived from a Focus on Speed.

The search for a uniform prescription for leadership competencies in today's environment will continue to be elusive—because no such remedy exists. Differences in strategic priorities, organizational cultures, customer requirements and competitive challenges dictate that each organization find its own way to identify and develop a cadre of strategic leaders. Transformational leadership will be one of the most difficult and exciting challenges facing executives during the turbulent decades ahead. However, of one thing we can be sure—teams will play an important part in future transformational leadership.

Chapter Eight

Team Leadership: Making It Work

Teams are tools.

Peter Drucker

What kind of teams do we need?

Many of us have ideal stereotypes of a perfectly functioning team, where cooperation was high and tasks were accomplished with a minimum of conflict. Maybe these memories are based on earlier successful experiences, possibly in the context of some competitive sport we played.

The reality of the business environment demands that we see beyond our ideal pictures of teamwork and begin to, as Peter Drucker has said, see *teams as tools.* In the hands of a skillful leader, teams can be utilized to accomplish a variety of different goals. However, team-building is often conducted in such a generic manner that there is no differentiation between the purpose of one team and the next. To use Drucker's metaphor, it is as if every team were being built as a hammer. If all we end up with is hammers, every goal will look like a nail. Building a house requires more tools than just hammers.

A leader must be like an architect in the design of his teams, determining the purpose before creating the design.

> ## Determine the purpose of the team
> ## before creating its design.

Far too often, organizations casually adopt a team structure and engage in team building without realizing the implications to organizational strategies, structural requirements, system demands and leadership capabilities. Teams can change an organization's culture.

To illustrate this point, let's examine the "businesses" in which different sport teams engage:

American football is a very strategic and tactical game where roles are highly differentiated: there is a defensive team, an offensive team, and a special purposes team. Every individual has a particular role to play—the kicker does nothing but kick the ball. Before every play, the team needs to communicate and agree on its next move. Each subunit is actually a team within itself, having its own well-practiced plays and roles to fulfill.

European football, or soccer, is different. The coach develops and implements strategy at the individual role level. All the players have basically the same skill set and can readily change positions. The person playing midfield libero today will initiate offense through the left and right offensive players, but tomorrow he may fill a different role, based on another team's weaknesses in defense.

Both "football" teams are entirely different from a baseball team, where the batter is individually responsible for certain results. Only when he hits the ball does team action begin.

Obviously, the kinds of interactions that constitute relationships within each team will differ according to the roles and responsibilities the members fulfill.

Sports metaphors about teamwork abound. These three are only reiterated here to reinforce the fact that leaders must determine the type of team needed for each specific purpose. Individual and team effort should be balanced for the team to be used most effectively. Role definition is where a leader can most influence the outcome of a team/goal change process.

> **"It's hard for a company to get out of its history. Old behaviors sneak back in."**
> **Paul Allaire,**
> **CEO, Xerox Corporation**

The planning of new team roles and behaviors is necessary but not sufficient to ensure a good team/goals change effort. The team's operating environment needs to change as well: leadership behaviors, reward and recognition systems, communication patterns, *other* teams' processes—all need to be adjusted to support the change.

Teams and organizational structures

The development of organizational structure and the design of a team approach should be considered simultaneously. Too often we attempt to gain the benefit of teams and team approaches without first dealing with old organizational structures.

> **First we design the structures.**
> **Then the structures take care of us.**
> **Winston Churchill**

The team approach never matched well with traditional functional hierarchies, which felt that they had very little use for teams. Team "meetings" were seen as ineffective, useless and a waste of time. Leaders did not believe in the effectiveness of teamwork, because all of their previous experiences told them that it wouldn't work in their organizations. Given the inappropriate match between teams and organizational structures in the past, it would be difficult to argue with them. The results spoke for themselves. However, what is rarely examined is the cause of team ineffectiveness in traditional hierarchies: *reluctance to change and leadership structures that were unwilling to share power.*

However, environmental pressures have forced companies to reevaluate the cooperative ineffectiveness of their old silo-type structures and move towards the more dynamic, empowered team approach. Creative solutions are not often easily accepted. Cross-functional teaming, with increased power given to smaller, independent business units is a threatening concept to traditional leadership.

Leader   Leader   Leader   Leader

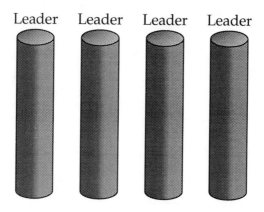

Figure 1: Organizational silos

The first, halting attempt to adopt a new approach was to re-structure centralized organizations into smaller business en-tities. Strategic Business Units (SBU) were formed, an at-tempt at *small within large*. However, when SBUs are mea-sured and rewarded for their quarterly, bottom-line profits, while simultaneously having to think and act globally, the resulting conflicts top the corporate headache list.

The traditional management solution to failed renewal ef-forts and poor cooperation between business units is to change the organizational boxes—alter the structure. More often than not this caused more problems than it solved. In fact, the frequency of structural changes was so great in some organizations that they were termed "spring/autumn" or "sponge-like" (expand/contract...expand/contract). Such frequent change caused accountability to disappear and made the organizations incapable of addressing real business issues in a sustained manner. More revolution-ary—and sometimes equally ineffective—measures were at-tempted, including downsizing and mergers.

Paul Allaire, CEO of Xerox Corporation, spoke of Xerox's education in the art of organizational transformation in the Harvard Business Review (1992):

> Typically, top management just moves people around or tries to shake up the company by breaking up entrenched power bases. Rarely do senior executives contemplate changing the basic processes and behaviors by which companies operate.
>
> Until recently, Xerox was no different. In the 1980's, we went through a number of organizations. But none of them got at the fundamental question of how we run the company.
>
> The change we are making now is more profound than we have done before. We have embarked on the process to change completely the way we manage the company. Changing the structure of the company is only a part of that. We are also changing the processes by which we manage, the reward system and other mechanisms that shape those processes, and the kind of people we place in key managerial positions. Finally, we are trying to change our informal culture—the way we do things, the behaviors that drive business.

Teams as transformational tools

Teams are excellent tools for organizational transformation. The complex interactions and strong emotional appeal of teams cause individuals to simultaneously develop under-standing of the team approach and commit to its success.

It's hard to commit to something you don't understand.

Even determined individuals find it difficult to change deeply rooted habits. Only when such a decision is sup-ported by other individuals involved in the change can good results be expected.

Change happens in teams.

When organizations attempt to restructure into *customer-driven networks* they must do an exhaustive evaluation of their place in the value chain and the changes that must be made to accomplish the restructuring goals. Only after an-swering questions such as, "Where do we really add value to our customers?" and "In which part of the value chain can we become the best in the world?" can organizations truly establish the mechanisms of effective change.

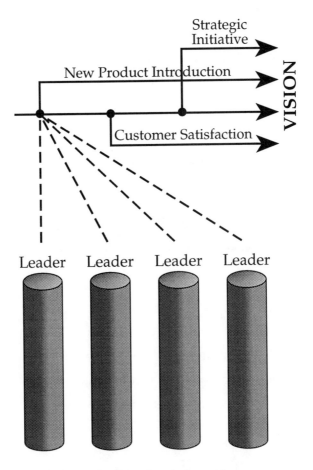

*Figure 2: Creating integration
with horizontal "customer-driven" teams*

The power of obsolete steering mechanisms

It is the rule, rather than the exception, that organizational systems are a step or two behind an actual change process. While the visionary leader is busy painting the preferred picture of the future and gaining commitment from the people, established systems and their adherents are continuing with business as usual, putting kinks into the change process. This has a major impact on success, and can be a rude awakening for the leader who assumes that all are being swept along in his wake.

> **Obsolete steering mechanisms turn market signals into useless noise.**
> **Roger Martin**
> **Harvard Business Review**

It is hard to hear customer needs when our focus is on internal turf wars. It is difficult to focus on external competition when we're busy trying to win internal battles. Traditionally, organizations have been "steered" from the inside, responding not to market signals but to internal demands. Companies are having to take their customers much more seriously.

Ten years ago Motorola introduced its Total Customer Satisfaction initiative in which *every* team has a customer, either internal or external. When a company's value chain becomes a chain of customer relationships, customer satisfaction is easily measured. Developing team structure around the value chain of an organization is a very effective means of providing the new teams with measured feedback and tangible purpose.

The effects of information and communication systems, which have always been bottlenecks to the development of any team-based approach, have been mitigated by advances in technology, particularly in the area of information net-working. However, unless more organizations begin to fully utilize the power of newer technology, these effects will still have substantial influence on change processes.

The tradition of rewarding individual performance is so deeply ingrained in our organizations that it often hinders implementation of effective team incentives. While team bonuses and incentives are designed to build *interdependence*, individual rewards are designed to promote *independence*. As uncomfortable as it may be, both followers and leaders must learn to accept team-based rewards as a part of establishing team-based systems.

Leading performance in a team environment

Most leadership models and theories have been developed to lead individuals, not teams. Being a rather recent development, there has not been much focus on the requirements for team leadership. And individual leadership continues to be of such great importance—and such a difficult task—that this lack of focus is understandable.

> **Leading individuals and leading teams are two similar yet different jobs.**

A leader's task is complicated by the addition of the team element, another possible reason for the reticence in establishing a team approach. Not only must individual leadership tasks be addressed, but the essential key processes and strategies for which the team is responsible must be factored in as well. Individual leadership has been a vertical process. Integrating teams requires a horizontal leadership approach. Horizontal team processes and goals will be elaborated on later in the chapter.

Matching teams and goals

The goal/team match represents the essential interplay between the goal(s) the organization has developed to help implement its strategies and the operating teams responsible for carrying out that implementation. A good goal/team match results in clearly defined roles and responsibilities for each team member.

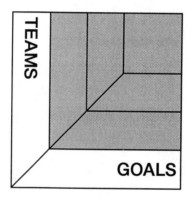

Figure 3: The second level of the Via Model

Although "teamwork" has been thoroughly covered in recent literature, the Via Model adds an additional element through the metaphor of "Tiger Teams."

Tiger Teams

The Tiger Team concept is an explanatory element of the Via Model. An intentional mixed metaphor, the "Tiger" refers to western peoples, who, like tigers, are individualistic and tend to hunt (compete) alone. But if they can learn the skills to act together, in "Teams," without losing their strengths, claws or stripes, they can be an unbeatable force in the jungle.

"Embracing the tiger" is an old Chinese phrase for an individual who is no longer afraid of losing himself. Each individual in a team needs to grow from independence to interdependence. Only the individual who trusts himself can trust others. Winning over interpersonal fear and daring to be genuine are the foundations for building strength and becoming a good Tiger Team member.

Tiger teams can develop when *three essential team elements* are adequately addressed:

Team Focus... The essential part of team focus is a vision that vividly describes team success. The team will have created the vital few team goals that everybody understands and to which everyone is committed. Also, everybody will have understood his or her role in the team and will have developed an individual focus by setting goals that are aligned with others' roles and the total team focus.

Team Play... Lack of communication and dialogue on a team is one of the most common problems for teams. Improving the situation calls for someone to take the risk to build interpersonal trust on the team. The one who does usually leads the process; more often than not, that person is not the formal team leader.

Team Process... When traditional processes stop working, and structural changes are made along with the introduction of team concepts, a re-engineering of work processes is also necessary. Often, re-engineering means making transformational changes in how the work is done such as increasing individual responsibility, delegating decision making power, introducing new skill demands, etc. Mapping out these processes is a way to make them visual and "discussible," effectively reducing the personal threats and confusion of change while gaining consensus about the entire process. Without consensus about processes, it is difficult to create a smoothly functioning Tiger team.

Goal setting in a team context

Unlike teamwork, the establishment of goals, both as a concept and as a process, has not been extensively addressed by either the academic or the popular press. The Via Model introduces a new approach that can make goals work, both for the individual and the organization.

In the traditional organization, goal setting was always a key process between a leader and his/her individual follower. In hierarchical organizations, where span of control was limited, this worked fairly well. Where the number of direct reports reached twenty or greater, the traditional approach was hard to execute and became overwhelming.

Goal setting has become a team exercise.

Several changes have outdated traditional MBO-systems and made team-based goal setting necessary.

Cooperation rather than competition... The horizontal organization demands cooperation between functions, teams and individuals. Traditional goal setting promotes organizational turf competition, rather than integrative commitment to horizontal partners in the organization.

When she became a candidate for the office of Attorney General, Janet Reno was asked by the Senate committee how she planned to promote cooperation between the FBI, the DEA and other government agencies. Her televised response was, "I think that these agencies are competing, instead of cooperating, because they genuinely believe that they have different goals. I plan to promote cooperation by establishing common goals." Reno captured the essence of the solution. However, the practical problem that leaders face is how to make it happen. Commitment to cooperation is not something that happens on command. Traditional vertical approaches to leadership will no longer work. Leadership is becoming much more a horizontal process.

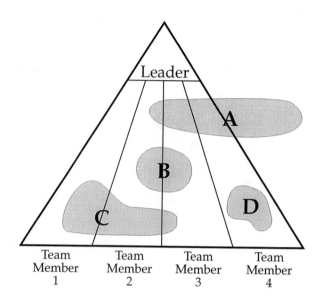

Figure 4: Tasks in a team structure

Tasks cannot be accomplished by a single individual... If a task is like D in the figure above, it is easily executed by a single individual, in this case Team Member 4. Traditional organizations tried to organize themselves in such a way that the work was in manageable pieces and the organizations themselves remained machine-like in their operations.

When tasks are more like B or C, a leader finds himself in the position of not being able to succeed simply by defining goals and tasks one direct report at a time. A team approach is needed. From an individual team member's point of view, it is essential that he get commitment from his colleagues at the same time that he gets support from his leader so that he is fully empowered to do his part.

Task A creates additional demands for cooperation, when commitments from another team also become essential.

Flatter, horizontal organizations call for a team approach... Teams do not function well in an organization if the members have not clarified their common goals and roles prior to setting their individual goals. The *process* of setting goals is different and particularly important in a team context. Communication and *real dialogue* can ensure that a common understanding of team goals and roles is shared by all, prior to execution of tasks. Leaders, who are accustomed to an MBO-style of goal setting, may feel rather uncomfortable when their roles change and the new team-oriented goal setting demands new skills.

> **High performance teams are committed to a common purpose and common goals.**
> **Jon R. Katzenbach &**
> **Douglas K. Smith**

The self-renewing team

In order to be most effective, a team must be able to function without constant oversight and input from leadership. A well designed team, with specific goals and clearly defined roles can become self-renewing—capable of adjusting to additional environmental turbulence and finding optimum balance through the feedback loops discussed earlier.

Dialogue and follow-through are team-based forces that energize the data from feedback and make continuous improvement possible.

> **Groups become teams when the members commit to a common goal.**

The Via Change Engine described in the previous chapter can be a source of continuous, measured feedback, dialogue and follow-through that constantly energizes the team.

How to develop an effective team

The question still remains of how effective teams may be developed in actual practice, how individual "tigers" may combine their personal talents to build team performance and transform organizational purpose into individual commitment.

> **How is organizational purpose transformed into individual commitment?**

Step 1: Develop the team's charter

It is important to create and view a team's mission or charter within the context of the overall organizational vision. Far too often, teams begin to see their own reason for existing as being more important than that of the whole organization. Maintaining perspective is crucial.

Step 2: Create the team vision

The power of vision is clearly visible at the team level. When a team has a clear and established vision, it has a co-ordinating focus that lasts beyond the immediate future and creates inspiration, enthusiasm and commitment. Establish the team vision from the outset, always within the context of the overall organizational vision. Everybody wants to be a member of a winning team. Vision paints what the "win" will mean to a team.

Step 3: Establish team enablers

With an established vision, the vital few critical elements that enable the team to achieve its vision are easily determined. Group discussion about these elements can be lengthy and frustrating without the central common element of team vision. The broad enablers that facilitate accomplishment of vision should be simple to determine.

Step 4: Defining team goals

Team goals are the arms and legs of team vision. The setting of team goals before the establishment of individual goals is particularly crucial. Inexperienced teams are prone to rushing the process, trying to establish goals for each member without translating vision into the vital few actionable team goals. Without the context of the team goals, individual goal setting becomes an exercise in management by objectives, resulting in competition rather than cooperation, unclear roles, unrealistic expectations, ineffective team processes and frustration.

The root cause for internal competition is the lack of common goals.

Step 5: Establishing processes and roles

Once vision, enablers and team goals have been established, it is necessary to sort out the numerous process issues that can plague teams if they aren't clearly dealt with. Relational issues between team members, between teams, and between functions should be made clear. Only then will discussions about individual roles have validity.

It goes without saying that organizational systems and structures must support the new team structure.

Step 6: Develop individual focus

Individual goals developed as a result of a team process are of the highest value and quality. Commitment level to accomplishment is highest when the team member *knows* that she is supported by others and that these others will also be accountable to do their part.

Traditional goal setting does not work in a team environment because team charter, team vision, critical enablers, team goals and roles are usually never adequately addressed.

Focusing on the end results of a team process is not enough. Goals must be set around desired *behaviors* as well. It is essential to "go upstream" in any team building process to influence the *inputs*, such as leader behaviors. In some "excellent" companies, up to fifty percent of executive bonuses are based on necessary leadership behaviors in support of change and team approaches.

Step 7: The extra step—
building individual commitment from the inside-out

Organizational goal setting systems are, by design, "outside-in" processes, with the focus being on individual achievement in the pursuit of corporate bottom-line goals. This is basically the structure described in steps 1-6. However, winning in the marketplace requires going beyond the competition. It means taking the extra step, walking that extra mile for the customer, creating the "little extras" that translate to memorable added value. The extra step in a team approach is the "inside-out" process that ensures that each individual is attuned to the team. Development of attunement, genuine commitment, internal motivation and the linking of personal gain to organizational goals will be addressed in the next chapter.

Why does a team process need to be tooled?

While a series of steps like those mentioned above create a checklist for the leader who wants to organize a successful team, you still need a method, "tools" that can be used interactively with team members to make the process work. We have developed *Via ChangeTools* for this very purpose. These ChangeTools, were built in the field with significant customer input and were designed to address the following issues in a change process:

- •Change causes pain
- •Change is difficult to manage
- •Two-thirds of change efforts fail
- •Speed is critical
- •Real change is personal

Our ChangeTools combine business and learning so that the people involved in the change process get the opportunity to work with "live ammo"—their real business issues.

Tooled change is a structured working process that will help an organization manage the pain of change, develop organizational readiness, creatively use teams as tools and create lasting change.

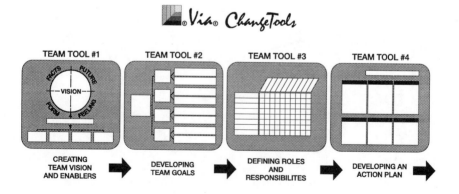

Figure 5: ChangeTools

A leader's steps in team development

In a team environment, every member is a leader who can influence others and have an effect on the outcome of team efforts. Therefore, the following three steps apply to everyone involved in the team approach, not just to those in formal "leadership" positions. These three steps are essential to good team process and final goal fulfillment.

Leadership step 1: Assessing readiness

Assessing readiness is a matching process in which a team member's readiness to perform in particular roles is evaluated against the requirements for those roles. Under traditional leadership models, this assessment would be conducted solely by the formal leader. In a team environment, all team members can provide accurate information about themselves and others, greatly enhancing the readiness defining process. It goes without saying that relatively high levels of trust are required for this process to succeed.

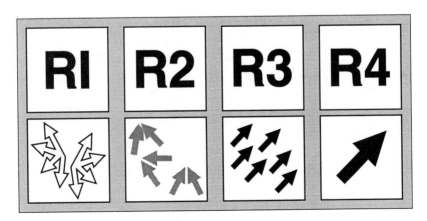

Figure 6: Readiness levels as icons

Leadership step 2: Making conclusions

There are structural differences in leading teams as opposed to leading individuals. Team leadership adds a horizontal dimension that must be addressed. Not only must *vertical* assessments be made, of individual team members in reference to their goals or tasks, but also *horizontal* evaluations of specific team goals or processes and the members responsible for their fulfillment.

To illustrate this leadership challenge in a team environment let's examine a four-member team (A, B, C, and D) having four team goals (1, 2, 3, and 4).

	Team Member A	Team Member B	Team Member C	Team Member D
Goal 1	R4	R4	R2	R4
Goal 2	R4	R1	R2	R2
Goal 3	R4	R2	R2	R4
Goal 4	R4	R3	R1	R2

Table 1: Readiness assessment of the team

Several conclusions may be drawn from this readiness chart:

- You need to assess individuals in reference to their roles (look vertically down the column), and to their common goals as they interface with the team (look horizontally across each row).

- Team member C will require your full attention. His readiness level is so low that performance without some assistance is not possible. He will need guidance and clarification of his tasks.

- Goal 2 is clearly where your input is needed. Few of the team members seem to have much experience and knowledge in this area.

- You might ask team member A to take a leadership role, especially in goal areas 2 and 3 where his readiness levels are high in relation to other team members.

- Team member B needs some individual leadership since his readiness level varies from goal to goal.

The example above demonstrates that it is worth taking a good look at your team, both from the point of view of individual readiness and readiness in broader critical success areas.

Leadership step 3: Delivering team leadership
Using this same type of team matrix, it is possible to design leadership strategies that match both individual team members' needs and team goal requirements.

	Team Member A	Team Member B	Team Member C	Team Member D
Goal 1	R4	R4	R2	R4
Goal 2	R4	R1	R2	R2
Goal 3	R4	R2	R2	R4
Goal 4	R4	R3	R1	R2

Tabel 2: Leadership by team member

- Use team member A as your co-leader.

- Spend additional individual leadership time with team member C, since readiness levels are low in all goal areas.

- Be prepared to take more clarifying and persuasive leadership actions with team members A and B. Given their relatively higher readiness levels, they do not need as much direct, individual attention.

- Team member D will be fine with organized support from other team members in Goal areas 2 and 4.

	Team Member A	Team Member B	Team Member C	Team Member D
Goal 1	R4	R4	R2	R4
Goal 2	R4	R1	R2	R2
Goal 3	R4	R2	R2	R4
Goal 4	R4	R3	R1	R2

Table 3: Leadership by team goal

- The team is high on readiness for Goal 1—
  let them run with it.

- You may wish to co-lead with team member A
  in Goal 2.

- There is enough readiness in your team to challenge
  them with Goal 3.

- Your personal focus is needed for Goal 4.

Tools for team leadership

Team leadership is a "process" rather than a "style."
Leading teams is like shooting at a moving target that moves
from goal to goal, task to task. We have therefore designed
two team *Leadership Tools* to help a leader orchestrate the
team leadership process.

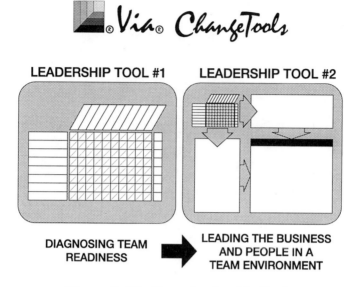

Figure 7: Via Team Leadership Tools

Leaders are in the follow-through business

As we discussed previously, follow-through is essential to achieving good results, particularly when behavioral change is the goal.

Follow-through is more important than goal setting.

This general leadership rule is no different in a team environment. Providing feedback, being willing to voice opinions, praising good work, capturing and multiplying best practices—all apply equally to teams as well as to individuals, and, in fact, have a multiplicative effect in the team set-

ting when more than one leader provides positive rein-
forcement.

The team leader's role as linking pin to other teams, functions, and higher organizational levels, is important. His coordinating role should escalate systemic problems, convey
needs, acquire necessary resources and provide constant
communication. He is a key enabler for his team.

> ## The team leader's role is to serve the team.

Team leadership requires skills over and above those necessary for good individual leadership. The multiplicative demands of teams may be intimidating at first, but, when ap-
proached in a systematic manner, can be broken into horizontal and vertical elements that make team leadership both
efficient and especially effective for today's flatter organizational structures. Good team leadership provides the building blocks for vision fulfillment.

Chapter Nine

Personal Transformation:
Via My Way

*There is incredible liberation
in realizing that you can
change your world simply
by changing your perception.*

Deepak Chopra

Careers in dilemma

We have seen how a turbulent and stormy business environment demands organizational change. When this occurs, individuals within those organizations must change as well, a challenging process at best. Basic givens of organizational life are in flux—careers that have been stable for years have become obsolete and expendable positions, the unwritten contracts between corporations and their people about employability and loyalty no longer hold.

> **In the 50's, one out of five ended his/her career in a managerial position. Now this ratio is one out of every forty five.**

We must begin to view career development and organizational life differently. New jobs are being born and old jobs are dying daily, requiring people to be flexible, to learn quickly, and to manage a life of relative instability and continual change. One can expect to hold between five and eight different positions over the span of one's career. This translates into a requirement for continual learning. However, as difficult as it may be to constantly keep up with technological and organizational change, it is even more difficult to change old habits and perceptions that are no longer valid and that, in the long run, can hinder our career success.

**Changing old habits and perceptions
is the most painful of educational processes.**

Leaving one's *comfort zone* will be a requirement for success in the coming years. New skills, new behaviors, and even new attitudes will be necessary. Those who are capable of responding to this demand as a challenge, who are willing to undergo several lifetimes of change compressed into their own careers, will have interesting and rewarding lives as they constantly look to the future. Those who cannot, who spend their time fighting change and get buried by it, will look to the "good old days" of the past and end up believing that life has betrayed them and left them behind.

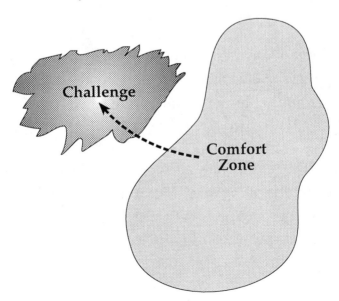

*Figure 1: Leaving your comfort zone and
accepting the challenge of life.*

Let's consider the move in Figure 1 for a moment. Assume that you are a 50 year old bookkeeper with 30 years of experience. Extremely competent and conscientious, you have a reputation for accuracy, even beating newer computerized systems with your old and reliable manual methods. And, proud of that reputation, you refuse to be trained in the new computerized methods, thinking that it will only double your work and force you to use tools with which you are not comfortable. When your workload increases as the company grows, you work more to keep up, finally reaching an exhausting 80+ hours per week, yet you are still not able to accomplish all that is put before you. Finally, after giving your utmost to the company, you are fired, a victim of your own inability to change. This example really occurred some years ago. You can imagine the frustration and pain felt by all involved.

In one form or another, this example is occurring every day as people rationalize their current behaviors and hold on to what is comfortable and familiar, refusing to change until a crisis point is reached.

New realities require new attitudes from those who want to be successful in the game. Motorola and General Electric have recently redefined the concept of employability, emphasizing *shared responsibility* for career development.

Motorola states that:

> **A person should be as employable on the last day of his/her career as he/she was on the first.**

This means making sure that the individual's competencies, capabilities and preferences match the company's requirements at all times.

Individuals must begin thinking like corporations, examining what kinds of services and products their customers (employers) want, both now and in the future, and taking steps to ensure that their knowledge, skill sets, abilities, and attitudes result in competitively delivered packages (themselves) of lasting value.

Self leadership— taking charge

> **Control your destiny or someone else will.**
> **N. Tichy & S. Sherman**

Taking complete charge of one's life is neither easy nor very common. When things do not go as planned or hoped for, it is very easy to blame circumstance, fate, other persons, luck, the recession, or something else that we perceive to be out of our own control. And these explanations may seem very plausible, often to ease our own pain.

The question is not one of whether we truly control every circumstance and situation of our lives, but one of attitude and inner programming that turn facts into perceptions.

Perceptions are created when we add meaning and interpretation to fact.

Our perceptions create our *reality*, evoke our feelings, and drive our behaviors. They are a product of learned responses and significant influences from the past—the cumulative history of our lives.

Inner programming is the product of our cumulative history.

However, perceptions are not absolute. Although a company may believe that its products and services are the best in the world, if its customers disagree, the business will suffer.

We should continually monitor the "fit" of our perceptions with reality. Without constant "reality checks," our perceptions create an auto pilot by which we *unconsciously* navigate our lives. We then become reactive to influences which shape our thinking and steer our behavior, rather than taking charge of the direction of our daily choices.

We should take charge of our perceptions.

Taking charge of one's inner programming and perceptions empowers action, enhances self-confidence, creates a future-oriented, self-motivating mindset, and truly leaves one in control of destiny and the future.

A date with destiny

When we set our minds to creating a vision for the future, we set a date with destiny.

> **At the moment of decision we shape our destinies.**
> **Anthony Robbins**

In actuality, relatively few people ever set a clear picture of the future for themselves. A number of studies have indicated that only between one and three percent of the population have actually set personal goals and have written them down. Less than twenty percent have even figured out the general direction they want to take their lives. A small percentage simply hope for the best, while the vast majority, over half the population, live in *silent fear* of the future.

In this era of downsizing, right sizing, corporate restructuring, capitol reductions, and change, there are, seemingly, plenty of reasons to be fearful. However, fear is an attitude based on perception. It is a thinking habit in which we have given certain meanings to particular events.

Fear is an attitude based on perception, a thinking habit.

The very same events that produce fear for some, cause others to envision opportunity. By taking courageous steps to overcome the thinking habit of fear, we can create new perceptions for ourselves, opening the future to positive changes we may never have imagined nor thought possible.

Leaving the "have to" world

An inner-directed, self-starting person does things because he *wants* to do them. A fearful, reactionary person does things because he *has* to do them. The more we feel we *have* to go to work, *have* to change, *have* to cooperate, *have* to relearn, the more powerless and disincented we tend to become.

Expressions such as "I should" or "I have to," affect us much differently than statements like, "I want to." The former produce stress, anxiety, and feelings of powerlessness, while the latter leads to a sense of achievement, enhanced self-confidence and a feeling of being able to control one's own life and future.

How many individuals in service or sales are constantly thinking, "I guess I *have to* serve my customers," and are actually satisfying their customers' wants and needs? Probably not many. However, if these individuals have had the opportunity to examine the personal consequences of good customer service, and, as a result, have developed an *attitude of service*, the likelihood is high that their customers are experiencing great service.

> **Rewards in life are directly related to the service we deliver to others.**

It makes all the sense in the world to take the time to examine the personal consequences of our actions and behaviors on the job, particularly those that affect the bottom line by our providing good customer service. Just as importantly, it makes perfectly good sense to leave the "have to" world for one in which we can control our future destiny and lead a challenging and rewarding life.

Your personal mission

Regardless of the job or type of organization in which you work, you are part of some subunit, division or team. As such, you have a role which others expect you to fulfill.

> **Your job is to add value.**

Under the best of circumstances, you and your associates mutually define roles and expectations for each member of the group. At worst, those expectations are never overtly expressed, and each person is left on his own to figure out the boundaries of acceptable behavior. Sometimes, the organization gets involved, providing detailed process engineering and training in group dynamics, but more often than not, it is up to each individual to establish those relationships that will enable him to achieve success on the job. Whatever the case may be, it is important for each person to define his or her *personal charter*: the role that *adds value* to the organization and gives the *reason for being* in that position.

> **You add value to your organization
> by fulfilling your role expectations.**

During a strategic planning process, an organization may ask such questions as, "What business are we in?" or "What is our mission?" Similarly, a team may ask, "What is our charter in this organization?" or "What is our goal?" Individuals must ask similar questions regarding their roles in organizations—What is my *personal mission* on this team and in this organization? The answer to this question is dependent upon *individual role and goals as defined by the team process*. Roles and goals provide the foundation for development of a personal mission statement.

Figure 2: A personal mission road

**Individual roles and goals
are the basis for personal mission—
the foundation for personal vision.**

The personal mission statement is the linking pin by which organizational roles and goals and personal visions are linked and aligned. Personal mission pulls together the purpose of one's job within the organization with the foundational personal vision that *integrates individual and organizational success*.

Developing a model
of personal transformation

Personal transformation should be an on-going process whereby individuals can positively and proactively respond to their changing environments. We often view transformation as a one-time experience or a stepwise process, when it should be understood and practiced as a continual adaptation. Within the context of organizational life, "effective" personal transformation facilitates a good match between an individual's growth needs, both career and personal, and an organization's survival and success needs.

There are two major elements to a personal transformation, integrally linked to one another. The first involves the structural or task elements of one's life, and may be viewed graphically as follows with vision being the central element:

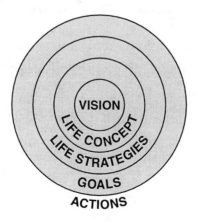

Figure 3: The structural side of the personal transformation model

The model's concentric rings, just like an onion, surround progressively deeper constructs of one's life. Actions are driven by one's goals, which in turn are motivated by one's life strategies. These life strategies stem from one's life concept which might be described as the balance, emphases and direction of life in total.

This structural or task element of the model contains the action-oriented, visible, planned aspects of life. An individual must truly "own" this portion of the model—understand and direct it—in order for plans to be actualized.

The other major element of the model may also be viewed graphically in concentric "onion" rings, which move conceptually deeper until anchored by vision. This side of the model consists of what might be thought of as the *software of the human mind*, those constructs that drive observable behavior. These need to be explored, as they are the primary components of personal transformation.

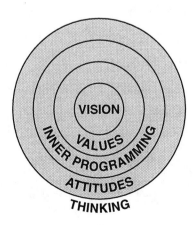

Figure 4: "Software" side of the personal transformation model

The most conscious part of the human mind is the *thinking* that steers our actions. These thinking patterns contain the skills and competencies that enable us to complete individual tasks.

Attitudes are a step deeper and incorporate our emotions and perceptions. Attitudes serve as programming, freeing us to attend to other matters, while they act as auto pilot. This, of course, may be both positive and negative.

Still deeper is the "operating system," our *inner programming*. Primarily subconscious, our inner programming may surprise us when we are faced with some environmental change that forces us to question that which we had formerly taken for granted as truth.

The deepest level contains core *values*. These core values are the strongest of influences, over which individuals have been willing to kill or be killed. Awareness of our core values is crucial to individual success. Without this awareness, decisions can be made that are contrary to our basic belief system, leading to confusion, stress and conflict.

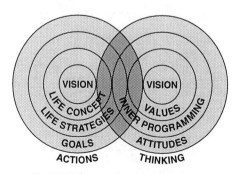

Figure 5: Matching the two major elements of the personal transformation model.

The model which we have developed to lead, manage and execute personal transformation is based on the match in Figure 5. Recognizing that the interaction within and between the major elements and their constructs is a complicated process, we have formed the Via My Way model.

Via® My Way

The Via My Way model is designed to help integrate the various internal and external elements of one's life to form the fabric which may be tailored into a personal life plan. By systematically weaving together one's plans, concerns, aspirations and dreams with the reality of organizational requirements, relationships with others may be seen more clearly and any "holes" or irregularities in the fabric may be addressed. The objective is to create a "win-win" situation for both the individual and the corporation, matching organizational survival needs with individual wants and desires.

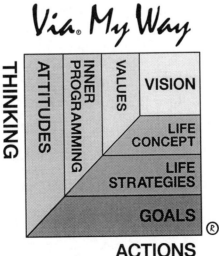

Figure 6: The Via My Way Model

The Via My Way model is based on the organizational Via model, and the same powerful integration ideas are applied to individual life.

Developing your personal vision

Your organizational role is related to the mission of the institution. By defining personal goals as a function of both organizational and team purpose, the essence of the organization is addressed.

Your future role with the company and your personal success, merge in your personal vision.

The whole brain approach mentioned in chapter 4, as applied to the setting of personal vision, maximizes the potential that the vision will be fulfilled. By appealing to all pertinent functions of the brain, a vivid "mind picture" of the future is created.

Vision acts as a guiding program for one's thought processes. It is a paradigm that influences inner programming, attitudes and perceptions.

Vision is an illustration of the preferred future.

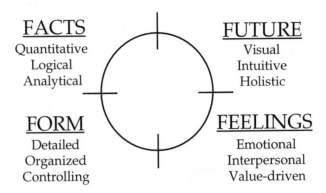

FACTS
Quantitative
Logical
Analytical

FUTURE
Visual
Intuitive
Holistic

FORM
Detailed
Organized
Controlling

FEELINGS
Emotional
Interpersonal
Value-driven

*Figure 7: A vision must address four parts
of brain functioning.*

Whole Brain Visioning

Whole brain visioning, as discussed in chapter 4, is revisited here for its application to the Via My Way model. As mentioned previously, four orientations of brain functioning must be addressed in the visioning process for successful fulfillment to be ensured. These are:

Future...A vision is a picture of the preferred *future*. As such, one must have a sufficiently detailed illustration of the future in order for the vision to have personal appeal.

Feelings... The image of the desired future must be emotionally anchored—we must feel good about it. That image must also be driven by values, and the pursuit of its fulfillment must be rewarding and fun.

Facts... The utilization of factual data anchors a vision to reality. Helping and hindering elements can be identified, and a realistic assessment of strengths and weaknesses can be conducted, further strengthening the likelihood of vision fulfillment.

Form... Form anchoring secures the vision to the "do-able." More process oriented than fact anchoring, form anchors address key measurements and realistic timetables.

> **The process of creating a vision is as important as the vision itself.**

Alignment occurs on the right side of the model

The right side of the model consists of structural elements that create alignment between your plans and your world, whether the focus is on your work role and goals or some personal aspect of life.

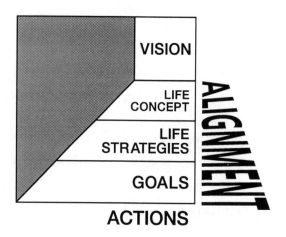

Figure 8: Alignment on the right side of the Via My Way Model

Let's walk through the different levels of the right side of the model.

The importance of a life concept

Life concept addresses the question of balance in life. Basic misalignments may occur, between vision and life concept for example, if elements are addressed separately. To create a seamless personal transformation process, elements must be addressed together. For example, a very aggressive career vision may never be realized if your life concept focuses on the enjoyment of free time, sailing, skiing and other outdoor activities.

By ensuring that your life concept reflects your values, balance in life can be maintained. It is very easy to lose this balance and then lose focus on that which is important.

For example, a *workaholic* may have enjoyed his job at one time, but, when problems appeared at home, he focused more and more on his work, simply because it was his *only source of pleasure and accomplishment*. Larger and larger "doses" of work were needed to compensate for the growing pain of his poor home situation, until life was thrown totally out of balance and he was caught in a no-win trap.

Life concept balance enables us to achieve our visions as well as choose appropriate life strategies.

Find your success formula by defining your life strategies

An important aspect of the Via My Way model is definition of life strategies. Personal guidelines for the implementation of core values, these life strategies make your life concept actionable. For example, if you value *integrity*, then some of the strategies you develop may include:

> *I always speak the truth.*

> *I keep all my promises.*

> *I never cheat on my income tax.*

Periodic clarification of who you see yourself to be and the principles by which you want to life your life is a useful exercise. According to an extensive study by James Kouzes and Barry Posner (1993), the most admired leadership characteristic is honesty, closely followed by competence, a future orientation, and inspiration. Do you, as a leader, value these principles in yourself?

> **A life worth living is one which we can look up to and admire.**

Strategies are the enablers of vision. They are the chosen ways of fulfilling our plans and guide the goals that we set.

Why goals alone will not make it

Setting life goals can be a difficult and frustrating experience, particularly in a workshop setting. Without a clear understanding of your preferred future, the balance you want to achieve and how to get from here to there, goal setting is not much more than the creation of a wish list for various facets of life—career, health, spiritual development, social, political, etc. Goal setting must be a coordinated exercise, anchored by vision.

> **Achieving goals is not difficult.**
> **Choosing them is.**

Everyone hopes that only good things will come their way in life. Very few truly anticipate the bad. Prioritizing what you wish to accomplish or achieve—and then truly putting aside those things you will *not* be able to do—can be very disappointing. Some refuse to set goals simply because this fact is too painful to face. However, prioritizing your goal setting is a conscious way of focusing your actions.

There are so many reasons not to act...

Human beings are very creative when it comes to finding reasons *not to act*. Even if vision is clear, all the planning is done and the goals are set, goal-oriented actions aren't guaranteed. Our "self talk" or "inner dialogue" consists of the many things we say to ourselves throughout the day. This self talk often determines the extent to which effort will be made to achieve set goals. Such talk may take the form of:

> *I am too old to do that.*
> *I am too young to be able to do that.*
> *I should have done that five years ago.*
> *Only a person with a college education can do this.*
> *I was born on a farm; I'm just a hick.*
> *I cannot speak a second language.*
> *I've never been able to do this before.*
> *It's a man's (woman's) job.*
> *Maybe I'll do it next time.*
> *It won't work anyway.*
> *I'll try it tomorrow.*

Pick your favorite excuse. A recent panel of graduating doctoral candidates advised their younger colleagues on how to expedite their educational goals. All of their advice boiled down to: *Do it now*.

Just do it.
Nike

By taking the first step, starting the process, you set in motion positive dynamics. A good start is an early victory; it creates positive emotion, motivates you to take the next step and boosts your self confidence to meet even bigger challenges.

The attunement side
of the model

Attunement occurs on the left side of the model, where our past history, experiences, and influences have the greatest impact. The probability of achieving internal alignment is in direct proportion to our ability to develop internal attunement.

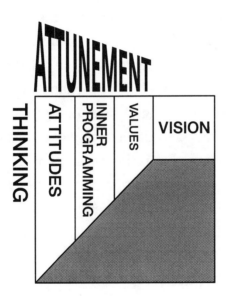

Figure 9: Attunement on the left side of the
Via My Way Model

New job requirements or changes in personal circumstances cause a person to develop new strategies, goals and/or actions. However, these action-oriented items will never be accomplished without first being processed by that person's inner programming.

> **A new goal has little or no chance of being realized if it contradicts with a person's inner programming.**

Logical goal setting, which is a part of the traditional managerial goal-setting process, never addresses a person's attunement with changes or new goals. It is just naturally assumed that people will cooperate. It is also assumed that substantial change will take a minimum of three to five years. Extensive implementation time is the *result* of lack of cooperation and ownership of a change process. Change must now be accomplished in a matter of months, not years. To accomplish this, genuine internal commitment and cooperation with a change must be developed. This commitment is developed within the arena of the *software of the human mind*, which will be addressed next.

Values are the core of a human being

Values have a strong "programming" effect on personal preferences, thought patterns, behaviors and subconscious choices. If one's vision is in conflict with one's values—if the picture of the preferred future contradicts with that in which one strongly believes, the results can range from vague dissatisfaction with life to true crisis. Dramatic and sometimes counterproductive changes—sudden shifts in careers, marriages, partnerships, or even suicides—may occur in people's lives as a result of the tension created by discrepancy between reality and values. Unfortunately, this tension often goes unnoticed by family and friends, and even the individual himself.

Inner Programming

Inner programming may be thought of as the paradigms or models which give structure to our values, and also which, because of past history, may be somewhat at variance with different aspects of those values. This programming is strongly informed by our experience and can lead to attitudes and thinking that are at odds with reality or that can create the future.

Although many persons believe that the paradigms of our inner programming are actually *who we are*, this is not so. Unlike values, which arise from the deepest parts of our beings, inner programming is the product of both who we are and that which influences us.

Identity may be the largest structure of our inner programming

Contrary to popular opinion, identity is *not* where our true selves reside, since much of our identity is assumed through environmental influence and education.

Many executives begin their careers in functional occupations such as engineer or sales representative. Years of education and experience in these roles can ingrain the identity of "engineer" or "salesperson" so deeply into their beings that future leadership prospects are inhibited. They become

incapable, because of entrenched *identity*, of seeing themselves as something else, and thus opportunity and talent are
lost.

Emotions

As with identity, many individuals mistakenly believe that
their emotions constitute their entire beings—"I'm just a
bundle of emotions..." Those who allow their emotions to
control them often rationalize their socially inappropriate
behavior as being "open and honest about my feelings."
Healthy individuals are aware of their own emotions, but
are not controlled by them.

Although it is good for us to be able to empathize and be
sensitive to what others are feeling, the mature person *does
not allow him/herself to be controlled by others' emotions.* Leaders
and helping professionals cannot become overly empathetic
without running the risk of losing their objectivity.

Inner programming is an important part of us and worthy of
continuous study in order to increase self-awareness and
make us more effective individuals.

> **If our life strategies and inner programming are out
> of sync, we have set ourselves up for failure.**

The importance of self confidence

Self confidence is also an important part of our inner programming, and can determine the degree to which we be-

lieve ourselves capable of accomplishing our goals and fulfilling our life's vision.

The Life Skills Map (1983) is a self-assessment instrument that evaluates 16 different areas of competency, such as communications, ability to manage change, assertiveness and time management. Self confidence was the one variable most highly correlated with success.

> **Self confidence may be the most important part of inner programming.**

Self esteem is closely related to self confidence. One of the most important things that a parent can help to develop in his child is good self-esteem. Children tend to have it naturally, but the difficulties of childhood and teen years can often steal it from them. These formative years are the most important for the development of self-esteem and should be guarded closely. Once lost, self-esteem can often take a lifetime to regain.

Attitudes as human software

> **Attitudes are emotionally charged thinking patterns.**

Good attitudes are the prerequisite to success, and provide the "programming" that can sustain a successful career.

Just as computers cannot function without the proper software, people become dysfunctional when their attitudes do not assist in goal achievement. Inner programming in the Via My Way Model is like a computer's operating system while attitudes are the software.

Attitudes are the software of the "Human" computer.

Attitudes can act like "auto pilots," causing us to react in specific ways because of past "programming." We must evaluate whether our attitudes help or hinder us from achieving our vision and goals. The key is to identify this auto pilot element. Once identified, we can make an informed choice as to whether we want to keep it or discard it.

Attitudes can be changed.

In the Via My Way Model, attitudes intersect with goals. As awareness of our attitudes increases, we can evaluate any possible mismatches between our stated goals and the attitudes that we carry which may aid or hinder goal achievement. Hidden attitudes—those of which we are unaware—will overcome conscious goals every time.

The most effective way to change other people's attitudes is to change yours.

Attitudinal change is difficult. We cannot cause others to change their attitudes simply by preaching at them, utilizing behavioral modification techniques, or increasing their extrinsic rewards. Leaders who have attempted these techniques, but who were not ready to change themselves, discovered the ineffectiveness of their efforts.

Attitudinal change begins with you.

Thinking precedes successful action

"Thinking" in the Via My Way Model incorporates much more than one's thought patterns or ability to process information. Included at this level—which intersects with actions on the right side of the model—are one's competencies, skill sets and accumulated knowledge.

Do you have sufficient knowledge and competencies to complete the tasks that will lead to goal attainment? Conscious actions are preceded by conscious thoughts. As work becomes increasingly "knowledge-based," thinking skills that are consciously honed will be of increasing value.

Matching the levels

The Via My Way process develops matches at four different levels, consistent with the original Via Model. However, in this context, *we create matches between who we are and what we need and want to do with our lives.*

Matching your thinking skills with action

The first match of the Via My Way Model involves the interplay between one's thinking and one's goal-directed actions. As mentioned in the previous section, knowledge, competencies and skill sets have a direct influence on ability to accomplish the critical tasks that lead to goal achievement. Within the context of the model, these interactions are viewed at a primarily conscious level.

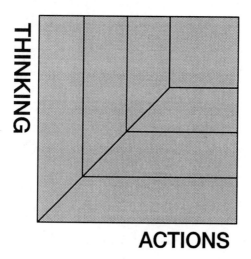

Figure 10: The first level of the Via My Way Model

For example, the sales force of a major telecommunications company developed a strategic initiative to streamline its order entry process. The old method was antiquated, inaccurate and labor intensive, so much so that it took weeks to generate a quote. The company's solution was to give every salesperson a laptop computer loaded with sophisticated software, capable of creating customized sales presentations and generating a quote within minutes. Now, instead of needing to ask the customer redundant and irrelevant questions, each sales person would be capable of knowing exactly what the customer had on site, what could be sold and what might be required in the future.

The business case seemed great, but the sales force was not ready to use the new technology. Their competencies related to the old way of doing business. Fortunately, 70% of them believed that the solution was simply a matter of training—on the thinking/action level, and they tried to use the new tools. However, 30% had resistance to use the new tools was at a deeper level, and their computers are now gathering dust. What a lost opportunity for both their customers and themselves!

Do your attitudes match your goals?

A person's success in achieving a given goal may be predicted by her attitude. As *emotionally charged thinking patterns*, attitudes are more consistent and reside more deeply in the human mind than conscious thoughts, so much so that we are often quite unaware of them.

Attitude indicates just how committed one is to a particular goal—the level of determination, competitiveness and persistence, particularly when faced with resistance. And attitude affects goal achievement so much that it is worthwhile conducting an *attitude check* prior to beginning the effort.

The response of, "See, I told you I couldn't do it," is often more indicative of attitude than it is of skill or ability. Attitudes affect goals as much as organizational culture affects strategies in the original Via Model.

Attitude influences the end results often more than talent or intelligence.

Leaders often make the mistake of beginning a change initiative on the wrong foot—they fail to process others' attitudes and feelings regarding the change effort and do not gain commitment, so many individuals start the process *believing that it will fail even before they begin.*

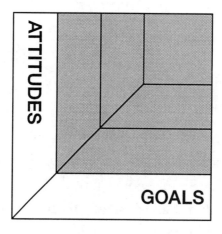

Figure 11: The second level of the Via My Way Model

Returning to our previous example, of the 30% of the sales force who believed their problem with the new sales tools was deeper than the skills level, a number of them recognized that they had very strong opinions and attitudes regarding the use of a computer as a sales tool. They made statements like "You lose the human touch," "the technology will fail anyway...," "it makes the salesperson focus on the technology rather than the customer."

**When you have an attitude,
you can rationalize almost anything.**

The bottom line is that *goals have no chance when attitudes don't support them.* This is why many goals never get realized. On the other hand, upon discovering an attitude that conflicts with a goal, you may use that goal as a tool to alter the attitude and achieve personal success. By taking charge of your attitudes, you take an important step towards taking charge of your life.

Working with your personal enablers

Life strategies has already been defined as those ways and methods we utilize to enact our life concept. The life strategies/inner programming match, as well as the life concept/values match, address deeper and more conceptual issues than those at the two previous levels. Our inner programming—self-confidence, self esteem, emotions, and identity—are directly correlated with the life strategies that we select, both consciously and subconsciously, to bring meaning to our balanced life concept. When the paradigms and models of our inner programming conflict with the strategies we attempt to utilize to bring life to our self-concepts, the ensuing mismatch nearly guarantees failure of vision fulfillment.

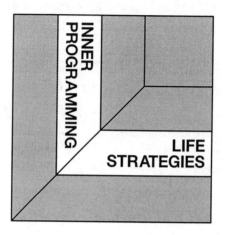

Figure 12: The third level of the Via My Way Model

The most important part of your inner programming is your attitude about yourself. Self-confidence is the primary internal enabler for achieving our goals and life strategies. Poor confidence greatly inhibits us.

We should learn to feel good about ourselves.

Everyone has his or her gift to give to the world. We all have a valuable contribution to make. We should be aware of our strengths and abilities and be ready to build on them.

Returning to our sales organization example, a number of the salespersons felt that their *identities* were "salesperson" not "cross-functional team leader" or "computer specialist." The older sales staff in particular did not *feel good* about the change, and, during interviews, indicated that they did not _feel confident_ to use the computer in front of their customers.

If the organization had chosen to proceed with implementation of this initiative, regardless of this feedback from the sales force, then a major _life strategy question_ would face each salesperson who was not comfortable with the change: "How can I still be a salesperson in this company?" "If the general trend is towards cross-functional team structures, should I bite the bullet and learn how to be effective in such an organization?" "Should I leave the company and look for a job where a 'salesperson is still a salesperson'?" "Am I resisting this change because I'm scared or because this change is not right for me?"

Issues become increasingly fundamental and personal the deeper one explores in the Via My Way model.

If there is no match between one's life strategies and inner programming, then even the finest career plan is just so much scribbling on paper. Addressing the issues and mismatches between a person's internal readiness and personal desires may be a very painful experience, but one that is bound to be beneficial. _Lack of awareness_ of one's inner programming may be the greatest stumbling block to progress.

> **Wisdom begins with seeing our reality**
> **J. K. Paasikivi**
> **Late President of Finland**

"Reality "is different from fact; it is *our* view of fact. J. K. Paasikivi was able to understand this when dealing with the Soviet mind, the inner programming of the leaders of a super power. As a result, he was able to establish policies that maintained the independence of Finland alongside its expanding neighbor.

Paradigm shift

The personal paradigms and models of our inner programming provide our frame of reference for viewing the world. They effectively program our attitudes, thinking and behavior.

Our personal effectiveness is very much dependent on how accurate our paradigms are. However, some of the most effective and accurate paradigms of the past are no longer valid. One only need remember our friend the bookkeeper from earlier in the chapter to see that this is true.

> **Old success formulas of the past hinder us from being effective in the future.**

We learn from our experiences, both successes and failures, and factor that information into future decisions and actions. However, we must be particularly careful not to allow patterns of success or failure to program our responses. Like the cat who, once burned, never jumps on a stove again, regardless of the temperature, we easily fall into patterned ways of thinking and doing.

> **Major change can happen very quickly.**

It is a myth that the bigger the change the slower it occurs. This is true to a certain extent, but when it comes to *paradigmatic change*, it can happen instantaneously. The value of currency or the price of a share of stock can drop instantly, based on new information. Macro changes are driven by changes in the minds of individuals.

When we voluntarily *choose to change our paradigms*, creating a better fit between our inner programming and life strategies, we can completely redefine our reality.

Value-driven life

The fundamental match of the Via My Way Model occurs between one's life concept and one's values. Here we are dealing with the most intrinsic elements of an individual— where he or she "lives." As mentioned previously, dramatic life changes occur when a mismatch arises between concepts and values. When addressed from a business or organizational perspective, a mismatch can result in inappropriate job behaviors, absenteeism, low productivity, poor quality, increased defect rates, unanticipated resignations, and/or emotional—or even physical violence.

Asking if your life is in line with your values is like asking if *you are really you*. However, the question is pertinent because external influences often force us to live and act contrary to what we value, resulting in imbalance, frustration and stress.

External influences that drive your life may disconnect you from who you really are.

Traditional management and leadership systems have always avoided the area of individual values and beliefs as "private." In fact, the benefits of deeply value-anchored commitment to an organization and personal attunement with one's work have been entirely invalidated as management or philosophical issues. However, many leaders have intuitively known the value of this type of commitment and been quick to tap into it.

In the Via My Way model, values are at the core of every being. We should be able to anchor our life concept to our deeply-held values so that the basic choices of life will reflect who we truly are.

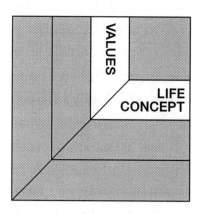

Figure 13: The fourth level of the Via My Way Model

Returning to our example of the sales organization, a number of salespersons felt that "fulfilling the quarterly quota" was neither in the client's nor the sales organization's best interest, and, in fact, posed a serious conflict with the company's published values of "satisfying customer needs" and "customer delight." Many experienced a serious values conflict between what they were asked to do and what they believed was right.

Many people never have the chance to think through nor articulate their personal values. Without that inner awareness of one's value anchors, it is difficult to define a vision.

The inside-out approach

Business organizations are autocratic, almost by definition. That is why the outside-in or top-down processes that proliferate in organizations are so much a part of every day life. However, well-managed companies are now integrating bottom-up processes with their top-down traditions. This both/and approach is the basis for Via My Way, providing an inside-out self leadership model to balance today's rapidly changing organizational structures.

Making it all come together

Alignment, attunement, level matching—is it all possible? Exploring the unknown, particularly one's personal unknown, is not something to be taken lightly, but which can produce significant personal gain.

People give plenty of reasons for not embarking on a discovery of their inner lives, may of which we have discussed. However, not doing so limits their potential and can be quite detrimental. Graphically, a life out of alignment and attunement might look like the figure below. It is easy to imagine what the consequences look like in real life.

Figure 14: A life out of alignment and attunement

Although the personal quest of using the Via My Way Model may at first appear intimidating, it can be both an exhilarating and challenging experience leading to greater personal significance, meaning and fulfillment.

Do you have
what it takes?

This question is asked not as a challenge, but as an *invitation* to self-reflection. Are your personal vision, life concept, life strategies, goals and actions aligned? Are your personal vision, values, inner programming, attitudes and thinking in attunement? Do you know what you aspire to over the next 48 hours, six months, five years, decade? Do you have what it takes to complete your personal Via Plan?

> **No one but you can change your "software."**

By accepting the invitation to self-reflection and taking the responsibility for your own inner development, you take the first steps to fulfilling your potential, both professionally and personally.

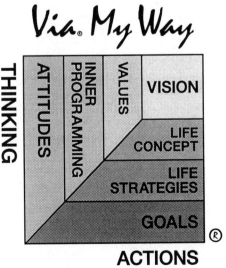

Figure 15: Your guide for taking charge

PART FOUR

THE CHALLENGE

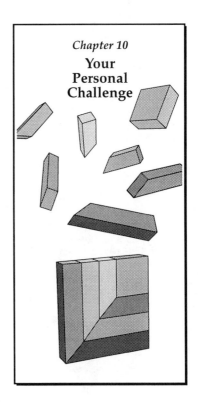

Chapter 10
Your
Personal
Challenge

Chapter Ten

Your Personal Challenge

He who does not want to improve,
is not good any more.

Seneca

What is the message of this book?

We began this book by saying that a *leader's job is to organize success*—whatever the circumstances might be. It has become clear that this job has become much more difficult and challenging; the pieces of the puzzle are more numerous and are not so easily assembled.

Figure 1: Scattered pieces of the leadership puzzle.

Without real leadership, an organization may end up looking similar to the figure above. Such discontinuity will be reflected in bottom line results.

The organizing principle of this book has been the Via, Vision into Action model. Leaders who walk through the book follow a *critical issues path* that can make or break their leadership efforts. We believe that the following questions, based on the model, will help you focus your actions and development:

1. How clear are your mission and vision in the minds of the members of your organization?

2. Is the business idea well understood by all key players?

3. Do your strategies and structures enable the organization to achieve its vision?

4. Do you "walk the talk" as a leader on visionary, strategic and team levels?

5. How good are you at designing transformation processes and leading change?

6. Do you know how your associates perceive your leadership effectiveness?

7. Do you know how to match organizational culture with strategies that will optimize implementation?

8. Can you rapidly organize a team and lead it effectively in a team-based environment?

9. What is your credibility as a leader?

10. What are your strongest capabilities? What areas are you working on to develop? Is your self-perception the same as that of your direct reports and your associates and colleagues?

The organization of success begins with you; only then will the pieces of the puzzle begin to fit into place.

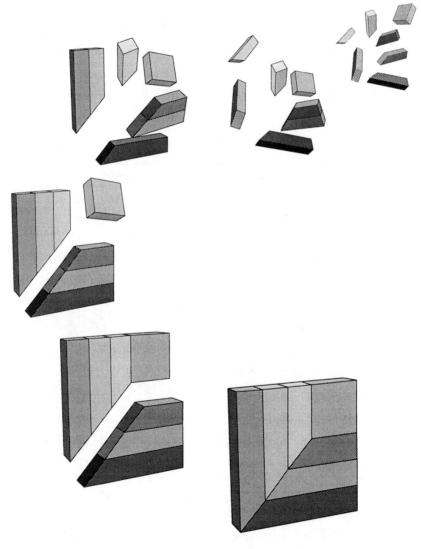

Figure 2: Organizing your success.

When will you be ready?

When your mission is defined, forming your chosen road to
success,

when vision paints the picture of your preferred future,

when that vision is anchored in genuine values and core beliefs,

when your key players give their support to a common
organizational vision,
interpreted for each function and team,

when developed strategies are real enablers to achieving the
vision,
and structures support the chosen business idea,

when organizational culture supports the strategic choices
and makes implementation possible,

when teams support their goals and have determined
their individual roles, responsibilities and
key processes,

when the systems are tuned to support the new structure,

when leadership at all levels drives and supports the process,

then you, as the leader, have done a remarkable job.
And now you are ready for the final stage:

when your management process meets the individual,
and you reach under his skin to touch his mind,
deal with his fears, understand his habits, address his
expectations—
even those that are contradictory or unfair,

when you begin to create real commitment,
to bring your people where they
never imagined they would go,

when your people are ready to take charge,
to win on their own,
to achieve more than even they thought they could,
to mature as human beings and
to be ready to lead others themselves,

then, my friend, you have done your job as a leader.

© 1994 Via Consulting Group

These words were inspired by the work of Rudyard Kipling. It takes a mature human being to be a good leader. Via is one way that can assist you on your road.

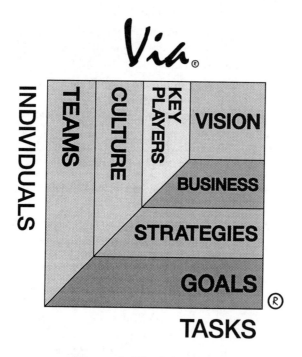

Figure 3: The Via Model

We hope that your leadership journey is a rewarding one, both for yourself and for those that look to you as leader.

Via Tools and Technology

What is the
Via Consulting Group?

The Via Consulting Group specializes in assisting organizations to manage large-scale change and complete organizational transformations. We have global experience developing *structured and tooled approaches* which can dramatically shorten the time needed for a change process.

Our approach is *visionary and strategic* yet *practical and results-oriented*. We *measure* the results of all projects, and are experts in the custom design of metric-based change initiatives.

The Via Consulting Network is a global association of consulting specialists whose affiliation is based on the use of similar tools and technologies. Via affiliates use the same *business learning* approach, which combines the virtues of both consulting and training into a practical, business-oriented process.

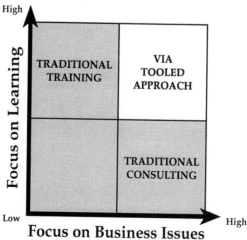

Figure 1: The business learning approach.

Good leadership is the critical ingredient to making change happen in organizations. Over the years we have developed a *deep understanding of the many styles and approaches to leadership* and how they may be used as drivers of organizational transformation.

How can we help?

When the business idea runs out of gas
Increased environmental turbulence and rapidity of change quickly outdate business ideas and shorten business life cycles, creating the need for new strategic direction.

The creation of new visions
The Via approach to vision creation is effective, value-based and resource efficient. We have assisted in the revitalization of businesses, government agencies, economic regions, local governments, health care organizations and non-profits.

Strategy development
New visions need to be implemented. The Via approach develops enablers that facilitate the implementation of vision.

The development of team-based structures
Organizing success in turbulent times often requires the development of team-based structures, which is a major emphasis in the Via approach.

Orchestrating cultural change
While the vast majority of leaders are working to change the culture of their organizations, most of them feel inadequate to manage that change.

Developing Tiger Teams

Via *ChangeTools* can assist in the development of effective and successful teams at every level of the organization.

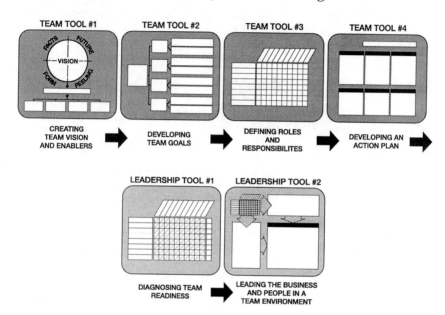

Figure 2: Via ChangeTools

Designing leadership

Via can guide the design and development of the criteria for necessary leadership behaviors at visionary, strategic, team and individual levels.

Our development processes and intervention approaches are custom designed for each client organization. The use of proven technologies and tested tools translates into successful organizational change and meaningful savings.

The interventions listed above are a sampling of what can be achieved using the Via approach. The Via model can also help you develop your personal leadership skills.

Receiving 360°
Via-feedback
from the people
vital to your success

Although we would like to believe that our evaluations are based solely on fact, leaders are deemed effective or ineffective based on how they are *perceived* by others. The feedback they receive is usually gathered in a piecemeal fashion, sometimes second- and third-hand.

The Via model addresses a number of issues, many of which are very conceptual, such as values, strategy and culture. Accurately extrapolating such data is quite difficult. Add personal information regarding beliefs and perceptions, and the water gets very muddy indeed. However, gathering accurate information about one's leadership capabilities is essential in today's changing business environment.

> **360° feedback covering
> all the aspects of leadership
> provides a leader with
> personal competitive advantage**

The composite picture of one's leadership abilities is formed by several perceptions. The Via Leadership Profile compares a leader's own self-perception with summary profiles from direct reports, associates, colleagues outside of his or her department or function and feedback from his or her own leader.

The results are presented in a 30-page summary report that compares feedback from each group with self-perceived leadership abilities. Statistical information and key indicators are combined in a graphical overview about the leader, and additional information, comparing the leader to others previously measured, is provided.

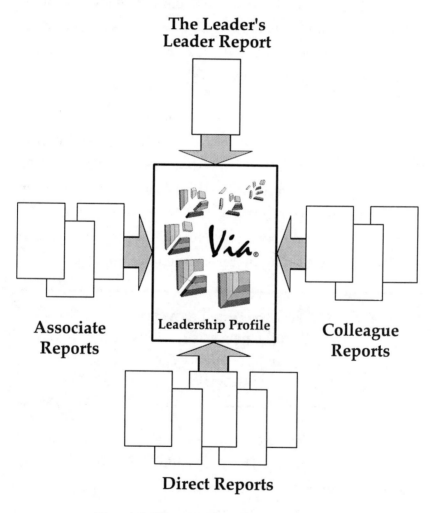

Figure 3: The Via Leadership Profile— summaries from direct reports, associates, colleagues, and your leader

Your Via Leadership Profile

The power of the Via approach comes from gathering vital information from all key players. This data provides the stimulus for examining leadership capabilities and making necessary changes.

Figure 4: Your Via Leadership Profile provides
a structured frame of reference for the feedback you receive
and maximizes the opportunities to reach your vision

We are interested in establishing long-term relationships with our clients. Your Via Leadership Profile is a way that we might get that relationship started. We would like to learn about you and your company.

If, after having reviewed the content and substance of the Via approach, you desire more information about conducting a personal Via Leadership Profile, simply complete and fax the form below, or call (619) 674-1900.

Information Request

Please send information about
the Via® Leadership Profile to:

NAME: _____

TITLE: _____

ORGANIZATION: _____

ADDRESS: _____

_____

_____

TELEPHONE: _____   **FAX:** _____

Fax or Mail to:

Via® Consulting Group

11440 West Bernardo Court, Suite 390

San Diego, California 92127-1644

Tel: (619) 674-1900

Fax: (619) 451-9914

Notes and References

Ansoff, I. (1979). *Strategic Management*. London and Basingstoke: The MacMillan Press Ltd.

Ansoff, I., & McDonnell, E. (1990). *Implanting Strategy Management*. (2nd Edition) New York: Prentice-Hall.

Ansoff, I., & Sullivan, P. (1993). *Empirical support for a paradigmatic theory of strategic success behaviors of environment serving organizations*. Unpublished manuscript.

Ansoff, I., & Sullivan, P. (1993). Optimizing profitability in turbulent environments: A formula for strategic success. *Long Range Planning*, <u>26</u> (5), 11-23.

Note: We have adapted Ansoff's scales as a means to illustrate the true extent of turbulence in the business environment. Although the scales are his creation, the descriptions applied have been developed by Via.

Argyris, C. (1993). *Knowledge for action: A guide to overcoming barriers to organizational change*. San Francisco: Jossey-Bass.

Argyris, C. (1982). *Reasoning, learning and action: Individual and organizational*. San Francisco: Jossey-Bass.

Balasco, J. A. (1990). *Teaching the elephant to dance*. New York: Crown.

Beer, M., Eisenstat, R., & Spector, B. (1990). *The critical path to corporate renewal*. Boston, MA: Harvard Business School Press.

Bennis, W. (1993). *An invented life: Reflections on leadership and change.* New York: Addison-Wesley.

Cameron, J. (Producer/Director). (1991). *Terminator II: Judgment Day* [Film]. Tri-Star Pictures.

Cappy, C. (Hollander, Kerrick and Cappy) Chris Cappy provided substantial information about the Work-Out process as practiced at General Electric.

Chapra, D. (1993). *Ageless body, timeless mind.* New York: Harmony Books.

Dansereau, F., Jr., Graen, G., & Haga, W.J. (1975). A vertical dyad linkage approach to leadership within formal organizations: A longitudinal investigation of the role making process. *Organizational Behavior and Human Performance*, 13, 46-78.

Drucker, P. (1993). Professionals' productivity. *Across the Board (CBR)*, 30 (9), 50.

Evans, M.G. (1970). The effects of supervising behavior on the path-goal relationship. *Organizational Behavior and Human Performance*, 5, 277-298.

Fiedler, F.E. (1967). *A theory of leadership effectiveness.* New York: McGraw-Hill.

Fleishman, E.A. (1953). The description of supervisory behavior. *Personnel Psychology*, 37, 1-6.

Frey, R. (1993). Empowerment or else. *Harvard Business Review.* 71 (5), 80-94.

Fuller, M. (1993). Business as war. *Fast Company Journal*, 1 (1), 42-50.

Goldsmith, M. (1993). *The impact of feedback and follow-up on leadership effectiveness.* (Non-published survey by: Keilty,

Goldsmith & Company, 4350 La Jolla Village, Suite 970, San Diego, California 92122)

Herrmann, N. (1990). *The creative brain.* Lake Line, NC: Brain Books.

Hersey, P., & Blanchard, K. (1969). Life cycle theory of leadership. *Training and Development Journal,* 23 (2), 26-34.

Hersey, P., & Blanchard, K. (1993). *Management of organizational behavior.* Prentice-Hall.

Hurd, G. (Producer), & Cameron, J. (Director). (1984). *The Terminator* [Film]. A film from Hemdale.

Jelinek, D. (General Electric) Dick Jelinek provided substantial information about the Work-Out process as practiced at General Electric.

Katzenbach, J., & Smith, D. (1993). *The wisdom of teams.* Boston, MA: Harvard Business School Press.

Kouzes, J., & Posner, B. (1993). *The leadership challenge: how to get extraordinary things done in organizations.* San Francisco: Jossey-Bass.

Leadership Studies International, (1992). *International Management and Leadership Survey.* (Non-published survey by: Leadership Studies International, 11440 W. Bernardo Ct., Suite 390, San Diego, CA 92127).

Lickson, J. *The Continuously Improving Self: A Personal Guide to TQM.* Menlo Park, CA: Crisp Publications, 1992.

Lickson, J., Kauppinen, T., & Ogg, A. Quality management: our multi-dimensional leadership challenge, *Hospitality & Tourism Educator,* 1994, 6 (2).

Life Skills Center, (1983). *The Life Skills Map.* Corpus Cristi, TX.

Long, D. (1993). *Competitive advantage in the twenty first century: From vision into action.* Australia: McPherson's Printing Group.

Lorsch, J. (1986, Winter) Managing culture: The invisible barrier to strategic change. *California Management Review,* pp. 95-109.

Martin, R. (1993). Changing the mind of the corporation. *Harvard Business Review,* 71 (6), 81-94.

Miller, M. & Hays, L. (1993, July 28). IBM posts 8.04 billion second period loss. *Wall Street Journal.*

Nohria, N., & Eccles, R. (Eds.). (1992). *Networks and Organizations: Structure, Form, and Action.* Boston, MA: Harvard Business School Press.

Pearce, J. II, & Robinson, R. Jr., (1991). *Strategic management: Formulation, implementation, and control.* Boston: Richard D. Irwin.

Porter, M. (1990). The competitive advantage of nations. *Harvard Business Review,* 68 (2), 73-93.

Prahalad, C.K., & Hamel, G. (May-June, 1990). The core competencies of the corporation. *Harvard Business Review,* 68 (3), 79-91.

Ready, D. (1994). Building a competitive capabilities profile: New roles for strategic leaders in dynamic organizations. Unpublished manuscript. International Consortium for Executive Development Research. Lexington, Massachusetts.

Schein, E. (1985). Organizational culture and leadership. In Schein, E. (Ed.), *Organizational culture and leadership: A dynamic view* (pp. 6-9). San Francisco: Jossey-Bass.

Schwartz, P. (1991). *Art of the long view: The path to strategic insights for yourself and your company*. New York: Doubleday.

Senge, P. (1990). *The fifth discipline: The art and practice of the learning organization.* New York: Doubleday Currency.

Stogdill, R.M. (1974). *Handbook of leadership: A survey of the literature.* New York: Free Press.

Strebel, P. (1992). *Breakpoints: How managers exploit radical business change.* Boston, MA: Harvard Business School Press.

Terry, R. (1993). *Authentic Leadership: Courage in action..* San Francisco: Jossey-Bass

Tichy, N., & Devanna, M. A. (1986, 1990). *Transformational leader.* New York: John Wiley & Sons.

Tichy, N., & Sherman, S. (1993). *Control your destiny or someone else will: How Jack Welch is turning General Electric into the world's most competitive corporation.* New York: Doubleday.

Vaill, P. (1989). *Managing as a performing act: new ideas for a world of chaotic change.* San Francisco: Jossey-Bass.

Vroom, V.H., & Yetton, P.O. (1973). *Leadership and decision making.* Pittsburgh: University of Pittsburgh Press.

Wheatley, M. (1993). *Leadership and the new science: Learning about organizations from an orderly universe.* San Francisco: Berrett-Koehler Publishers.

Yukl, G. (1989). Managerial theory: A review of theory and research. *Journal of Management*, 15 (2), 251-289.

Zaleznik, A. (May 1977). Managers and leaders: Are they different? *Harvard Business Review*, 55 67-78.

Index